Business Communication Skills

Business Communication Skills

Consultant Editor
MEETA GHOSH

The Pearson–ICFAI University Series is an outcome of a collaboration between Pearson Education India and ICFAI University Press.

PEARSON

Delhi • Chennai • Chandigarh

Acquisitions Editor: Prasun Chatterjee
Assistant Production Editor: Sonam Arora

ISBN 978-81-317-6140-3

First Impression

Published by Dorling Kindersley (India) Pvt. Ltd, licensees of Pearson Education in South Asia.

Head Office: 7th Floor, Knowledge Boulevard, A-8(A), Sector 62, Noida, UP 201309, India.
Registered Office: 11 Community Centre, Panchsheel Park, New Delhi 110017, India.

Compositor: White Lotus Infotech Pvt. Ltd, Puducherry
Printer: Saurabh Printers Pvt. Ltd.

Contents

About the Editor

Meeta Ghosh teaches business communication and personality enhancement to undergraduates and post graduates of Business Administration, Retail, Marketing and Human Resource Management at the Institute of Management Sciences, Lucknow University. Earlier, she has taught business communication at the Institute of Hotel Management Lucknow for more than a decade. She holds a doctoral degree in English literature from Lucknow University.

1

Fundamentals of Communication

In this chapter, we will discuss:

- The Importance of Communication
- The Basic Forms of Communication
- The Process of Communication
- Barriers of Communication
- Dealing with Communication Barriers

Communication is the process of transferring meanings. In a business setting, this process sometimes accounts for the difference between success and failure and also profit and loss. This fact is now being recognized by both the corporate community and business schools. In a 1984 Harvard Business Review poll of practitioners and academicians, both groups felt that the oral and written skills of MBAs required a great deal of improvement.

Today, business communication has become so important that many colleges and universities, nationally and internationally, require the course for graduation. It is becoming clear to all the concerned parties that communication is critical to the effective functioning of modern business enterprises.

THE IMPORTANCE OF COMMUNICATION

Effective business communication is important both to the individual and to modern organizations.

Helping You

Good communication skills often make the difference between being hired and fired. A well-written resume and cover letter, and a convincing interview, can get you the job you want even though more qualified people had applied for it.

Receiver

The receiver is the individual to whom the message is directed. The extent to which this person comprehends the message will depend on a number of factors, including: (i) how much the individual knows about the topic, (ii) his receptivity to the message, (iii) the relationship and trust that exists between sender and receiver, and (iv) the receiver's understanding and perception of the information being conveyed.

Perception refers to an individual's view of reality. It is the result of many factors, including past experience, attitude towards the message and the sender, mental abilities such as intelligence, and communication skills such as speaking and listening. It is important to realize that a person's perception is not always accurate.

Feedback

Feedback is the receiver's response to a message; it can take a number of verbal and nonverbal forms. In verbal form, some of the most common responses are designed to obtain more information or to provide closure by letting the sender know that the message has been received and will be acted upon accordingly. Following are some examples.

For getting more information:

- 'Your idea sounds good, but how will it help increase work productivity?'

Providing closure:

- 'I will get started on this right away and have the report on your desk by next Friday'.

Feedback also reveals attitude, perception and comprehension or lack of it. In nonverbal form, some of the most common examples of feedback are nodding one's head, shrugging, grimacing, smiling, winking, rolling one's eyes, looking the other person directly in the eye and looking away from the other person.

BARRIERS TO COMMUNICATION

There are many types of communication barriers. For the purpose of analysis, they can be placed into four categories: problems caused by the sender, problems in message transmission, problems in reception, and problems in receiver comprehension and perception.

Problems Caused by the Sender

The sender is the individual who encodes the message. A number of barriers can prevent this individual from properly handling a communication task. One is the amount of information the individual has about the subject of the message.

Too much knowledge about the subject can also be a problem. The sender may over explain the message or make it so detailed and complex that it is confusing. A third barrier is indecision regarding selection of information. What should be included? What should be left out? Until the sender can answer these questions, he will be unable to complete the message.

A fourth barrier is the order of presentation. What should be presented first? What should come next? It is often a good idea to present some general material first to set the stage for the material to follow. For example, if a series of productivity improvement recommendations are being presented to the manager, they should be preceded by a discussion of the current productivity situation and an analysis of the causes of low productivity.

A fifth barrier is a lack of familiarity with the audience. A sender who does not know the audience very well may use an inappropriate approach. For example, if the audience does not know much about the subject, a brief discussion is in order. The message should also be conveyed in a carefully structured format that presents the information in an easy-to-understand manner. On the other hand, if the audience is knowledgeable about the subject, the sender should move immediately to the heart of the matter and present the important information upfront. A sender who is unfamiliar with his audience is likely to confuse the first group and disinterest the second.

A sixth barrier is a lack of experience in speaking or writing. When senders have limited education or training in communication, they often have difficulty expressing their ideas. Their vocabulary is limited, their word choice is poor, there are punctuation and spelling errors and the overall presentation style is ineffective.

Problems in Message Transmission

Communication can also break down because of problems in transmission. One major problem is the number of transmission links. When a verbal message is transmitted through three or four different people before reaching its final destination, the message will most likely be altered or changed through the stages in communication. This distortion of message occurs often in upward and downward communications.

Another major problem is the transmission of unclear or conflicting messages. When a message contains two confliction parts, the receiver may have trouble dealing with the communication. Consider, for example, a memo to the head of the shipping department that directs him to immediately reduce shipping costs while ensuring that all deliveries are made in an expeditious manner. The message appears to be contradictory. How can the manager cut costs and still ensure that all deliveries are made quickly?

Problems in Reception

Sometimes there are communication problems because of problems in reception. Communication scholars use the term 'noise' to refer to factors that interfere with the exchange of messages. 'Physical noise'—external sounds that distract communicators—falls into this category but that are other types of external noise that cannot involve sound. For example, an overcrowded room or a smelly cigar can disrupt concentration. A second kind of interference is caused by physiological noise. Hearing disorders fall into this category, as do illnesses and disabilities that make it difficult to receive messages. The third type of interference is 'psychological noise', which consists of forces within the receiver that interfere with understanding—egotism, defensiveness, hostility, preoccupation, fear and so on.

Problems in Receiver Comprehension

Sometimes the receiver will have a problem comprehending the message. There are a number of reasons for this. One is that he may not understand some of the words being used. This is a common problem when a company or industry uses technical terms that have special meaning for them. For example, in engineering firms, the term 'burn' means to 'make a photocopy'. In the medical sciences, 'OB' refers to obstetrics, while in management studies, it refers to 'organizational behaviour'.

DEALING WITH COMMUNICATION BARRIERS

The following section analyzes different communication situations, but they all have one common focus: how to deal with communication barriers. Although each communication situation is unique, there are some basic methods for dealing with communication barriers. In this section, we discuss these methods, and in subsequent chapters we will refer to or repeat them.

Know Your Subject

Identify the topic you are going to discuss and find out (may be even research) all you need to know about it. In particular, find out all the important, specific details, because without details it is not possible to guide or instruct anyone clearly.

At the same time, the writer or speaker should be clear about what he wishes to convey and select the material accordingly.

Focus on the Purpose

To determine the type and amount of information you should include in your document (or presentation), you should know the purpose of your message. If you are writing a report on the consumer market for sports equipment but you do not know the purpose of the report, it would be hard to determine what to include or exclude from the report.

Know Your Audience

To convey your purpose effectively, you must know about and understand your audience. You need to know something about the biases, education, age and status of your receiver to create an effective message. Decisions about the content, organization, style and tone of your message all depend, at least to some extent, on the relationship between you and your audience. If you do not know your audience, you will be forced to make these decisions in the dark, and your message, or at least part of it, will not be conveyed effectively.

By examining the message from the other person's point of view, the sender can identify some of the problems to be encountered and can work to sidestep or minimize them.

Be Organized

Knowledge of the subject, purpose and audience will also help you to organize your material in such a way that it conveys your message effectively. For example, if the receiver is not familiar with the subject, you might have to first give some background information.

Communication should be organized in such a way that it conveys the sender's message effectively. This means that the communication should be structured in such a way that it is easily readable by and understandable to the audience.

About This Book

Different in many ways, the fundamental rules of communication hold true for both. As a result, there is some necessary overlap between both parts of the book.

The second part of the book provides numerous examples and guidelines to enable readers to think for themselves and learn to adapt to different writing situations. As with the first part, the purpose is not to prescribe rules, but to 'enable' the readers. In this fast-changing world, it is important to grasp the 'tools' and not the 'rules' of communication.

The building blocks of communication, however, do not change. That is why this book concludes with a review of writing skills: sentence structure, paragraph structure and composition.

2

Nonverbal Communication

In this chapter, we will discuss:

- Characteristics of Nonverbal Communication
- Components of Nonverbal Communication

A

Your boss has been telling the staff that he would welcome suggestions about how to improve the organization. You take him at his word and meet him to discuss some of your ideas with him. As you begin to outline the changes you propose, he fixes you with an icy stare and folds his arms across his chest; as you go on, the frown on his face gathers intensity. When you finish, he gets up abruptly and says, with barely suppressed menace in his voice, 'Thank you very much. Your ideas are priceless'.

B

Your friend has started a new organization. He is encountering some labour problems. You are a personnel management specialist and have several years of experience in the personnel department of a large conglomerate. Your friend calls you over to his office one day to discuss his problems. In the course of the conversation, you give him some ideas about how he could solve his problems. He finds your ideas innovative and thinks they are just right for his kind of set-up. As you get up to leave, your friend clasps your hand warmly, beams at you and says, 'Thank you very much. Your ideas are priceless'.

Thus, though his words say something different, what he actually says is: '*You have a nerve, coming in here and trying to tell me how I should run this place*'.

Communication researchers have found that nonverbal signals have more impact in conveying meaning than verbal content. In fact nonverbal behaviour is so important to effective business communication that many companies are now trying to train their employees to understand it.

CHARACTERISTICS OF NONVERBAL COMMUNICATION

We have seen how nonverbal signals can completely alter the message that you communicate. Let us now look at some of the characteristics of nonverbal communication.

- **Nonverbal messages primarily communicate emotions, attitudes:** Nonverbal signals largely communicate a person's subjective response—anger, appreciation, dislike, resentment—to a particular situation. Messages about ideas or concepts cannot be conveyed through nonverbal channels. For instance, if you want to give your friend the message, 'The sales meeting is coming up next Monday', there is no way you can do this using nonverbal signals. However, you can express you attitude to the 'sales meeting'—dread, eager anticipation—through nonverbal signals.
- **Nonverbal cues substitute for, contradict, emphasize or regulate verbal messages:** If someone asks you which way the MD's room is, you may simply point down the corridor. You may praise your friend's new dress while your face shows absolute dismay, or you may use your hands to indicate the monstrous proportion of somebody's ego. Very often we regulate the flow of conversation nonverbally by raising an index finger, nodding and leaning forward, raising eyebrows and/or changing eye contact.
- **Nonverbal cues are often ambiguous:** Nonverbal cues are not always easy to understand. Their meaning varies by culture and context. Sometimes they convey meanings that were never intended. A random gesture may be assumed to have meaning when none at all was intended. On the other hand, some people may feel emotion strongly, but find that their bodies do not respond appropriately.
- **Nonverbal cues are continuous:** It is possible to stop talking, but it is generally not possible to stop sending out nonverbal cues. The attempt to mask one's communication communicates something in itself. Long periods of silence at the supper table communicate as clearly as any words that something may be wrong.
- **Nonverbal cues are culture bound:** Many nonverbal gestures are universal. Most human beings, no matter what culture they belong to,

smile when happy and frown when unhappy. But certain nonverbal expressions vary from culture to culture. Gestures seen as positive in one culture may be seen as obscene in another culture.

COMPONENTS OF NONVERBAL COMMUNICATION

The study of nonverbal signals is divided into three main areas: paralanguage, the way we say what we say; kinesics, the study of body language and facial expression; and proxemics, which is the study of how physical space is used.

Paralanguage

The study of paralanguage focuses on how you say what you say. The tone of our voice, the loudness and softness rate of speech, and the words we accentuate communicate a great deal. In fact, by changing the emphasis in a sentence, we can change the total meaning of the sentence. Paralanguages have several component parts: voice qualities, voice quantity, characteristic individual work.

Voice Qualities

Voice qualities include such as cottage rate of speech price pronunciation and enumeration.

Volume

A person may sometimes speak louder to attract others' attention. On the other hand, though a soft voice conveys a sense of calm, in a business setting it may give an impression of weakness or indecisiveness. Thus, the volume that may be right in one setting may convey a negative message in a different situation.

Rate of Speech

Fast speech often makes people nervous, while slow speech causes boredom or leads people to believe that the speaker is not quite sure about what to say next.

Voice Pitch

Voice pitch is often equated with emotion. High pitch shrieking generally indicates excitement or nervousness. A low voice pitch usually commands attention and respect, because it indicates that the speaker is in control of the situation.

Box 2.1

Head shakes are particularly difficult to interpret. People in the United States shake their heads up and down to signify 'yes'. Many British, however, make the same motions just to indicate that they hear—not necessarily that they agree. To say 'no', people shake their heads from side to side in the United States, jerk their heads back in a haughty manner in the Middle East, wave a hand in front of the face in the Orient and shake a finger from side to side in Ethiopia.

The pointing of a finger is a dangerous action. In North America, it is a very normal gesture, but it is considered very rude in many other parts of the world—especially in areas of Asia and Africa. It is therefore much safer to merely close the hand and point with the thumb.

Other forms of communication have also caused problems. The tone of the voice, for example, can be important. Some cultures permit people to raise their voices when they are not close to others, but loudness in other cultures is often associated with anger or loss of self-control.

A lack of knowledge of such differences in verbal and nonverbal forms of communication has resulted in many a social and corporate blunder. Local people tend to be willing to overlook most of the mistakes of tourists; after all, they are just temporary visitors. Locals are much less tolerant of the errors of business people—especially those who represent firms trying to project an impression of permanent interest in the local economy. The consequences of erring, therefore, are much greater for the corporation.

Source: David A. Ricks, *Big Business Blunders.*

Rhythm

Rhythm refers to the pattern of the voice. A smooth rhythm, like a moderately low pitch, indicates a confident, authoritative attitude, while an uneven rhythm may convey lack of prior preparation and lack of clarity.

Pronunciation and Enunciation

Good pronunciation is the correct oral delivery of a word. While enunciation is more a matter of clear articulation. People with poor enunciation drop word endings, slur their speech or do not speak clearly. Poor enunciation may indicate carelessness, but overly precise enunciation may sometimes seem affective.

Voice Qualifiers

Temporary variations in pitch, volume and rate of speech are known as voice qualifiers.

Vocal Characteristics

All of you are familiar with certain audible sounds like sighing, laughing, crying, clearing the throat, whistling and groaning, whereas sounds that serve to communicate some meaning are called vocal characteristics. As a communication expert put it: 'Awareness of the more subtle voice characteristics, such as pleasantness, especially in combination with voice qualifiers, can do much to help individuals and organizations improve communication'.

Vocal Segregates

Meaningless words or sounds such as 'er', 'um' are used to punctuate or pace the sentence and are called vocal segregates. Filler expressions like 'right?' 'you know what I mean' or 'OK' are used to fill in their silences. Vocal segregates are usually awkward components of speech and should be avoided as far as possible. These sounds indicate a lack of confidence and exhibit a feeling of stress on the part of the speaker.

Kinesics

Kinesics is the study of facial expressions and body language.

The way people sit or stand reveal a lot about their attitudes and emotions. Posture portrays confidence, anxiety, fear, aggressiveness and a host of other emotions. A boss who wants to reprimand his subordinate may do so by standing, leaning over the table and peering down at the hapless employee. Here, he is using posture to establish his superiority.

Gestures

Gestures are of various types as detailed in Box 2.2.

There are gestures that have a meaning and are understood by the public at large. Sometimes the same gesture may have different meanings in different cultures. For instance, forming an 'O' with index and thumb means 'OK' in the United States. While in Japan it means 'money' and in parts of France it means 'worthless' or 'zero'.

These are learned behaviour patterns that we usually pick up in childhood. The way we use our spoons or our hands while eating is a good example.

Box 2.2: How Do Facial Expressions Convey Meaning?

- **Surprise:** The eyebrows are raised, the eyes are opened wide, and the jaw drops open, parting the lips.
- **Fear:** The eyebrows are raised and drawn together, the eyes are open and the lower lid is tensed, the lips are stretched back.
- **Disgust:** The upper lip is raised, while the lower lip may be raised or lowered, the nose is wrinkled, the lower eyelids are pushed up, and the eyebrow is lowered.
- **Anger:** The eyebrows are lowered and draw together, the eyelids are tensed and the eye appears to stare in a hard fashion. The lips are either tightly pressed together or parted in a square shape.
- **Happiness:** The corners of the lips are drawn back and up. The mouth may or may not be parted. Crow's feet wrinkles go outward from the outer corners of the eyes.
- **Sadness:** The inner corners of the eyebrows are raised and may be drawn together.

The corners of the lips are drawn down or the lips appear to tremble.

Again, there are gestures that go with what we are saying verbally and tend to depict what is being said. A good example is when you tell someone, 'Come, sit in this chair' and accompany it by a nod of the head or a wave of the hand.

These are again gestures that control the communication exchange. Patting an employee on the back may encourage him to keep talking. Shuffling through your papers while he is talking will certainly encourage him to stop.

Facial Expressions

The face plays a vital role in communicating various messages. The brow, the eyes, the root of the nose, the lower face are all capable of conveying attitudes and emotions. For example, to express surprise one raises his eyebrows and opens his eyes wide. Similarly, fear is expressed with raised eyebrows and tensed facial expression. As a matter of fact, eye contact varies by culture. For instance, some Latin American cultures teach children not to look directly at the face of an adult, whereas avoiding eye contact indicates nervousness, embarrassment or humiliation.

Proxemics

Proxemics is the study of how people use the physical space around them and what this use says about them. People often put an invisible boundary between themselves and others. This is called the personal feature space. For example, the intimate distance zone within a radius of up to 18 inches around a person is reserved for close relations and friends.

The social distance zone extends from 4 to 12 feet. It is in this zone that most business is transacted. The public distance zone usually extends from 12 to 25 feet. Thus, by observing the physical distance between two individuals, one can judge the relationship between them.

Note that in organizations, the control of space generally constitutes an extension of one's personal power. Status can often be determined by how much space a person occupies. The more status a person has, the easier it is for him or her to invade someone else's space. For instance, it is all right for a manager to walk into a subordinate's office, but the subordinate must seek permission to enter the manager's room.

If your actions belie your words there's every possibility the listener may choose to believe your actions, rather than your words.

3

Listening

In this chapter, we will discuss:

- The Importance of Listening
- Barriers to Effective Listening
- Approaches to Listening
- How to Be a Better Listener
- What Speakers Can Do to Ensure Better Listening

THE IMPORTANCE OF LISTENING

Listening is the most frequent, perhaps the most important type of communication. Studies indicate that adults spend about 29.5 per cent of their waking hours listening. Recent studies that focus on the workplace show that, on an average, personnel at all levels spend about 32.7 per cent of their time listening, while speaking takes up 25.8 per cent of their time and writing 22.6 per cent. Top executives spend even more time listening than other employees.

In fact, most managers agree that 'active listening' is the most crucial skill for becoming a successful manager because it improves work quality and boosts productivity. Poor listening leads to innumerable mistakes because of which letters have to be retyped and meetings rescheduled; besides, listening helps employees to update and revise their collection of facts, skills and attitudes and also improves their speaking skills.

BARRIERS TO EFFECTIVE LISTENING

When we hear, we only perceive sounds, but when we listen, this hearing is accompanied by a deliberate and purposeful act of the mind. To listen means to get meaning from what is heard. One may hear the words another person utters without really understanding them. There are many factors that impede effective hearing. Figure 3.1 outlines some of these barriers.

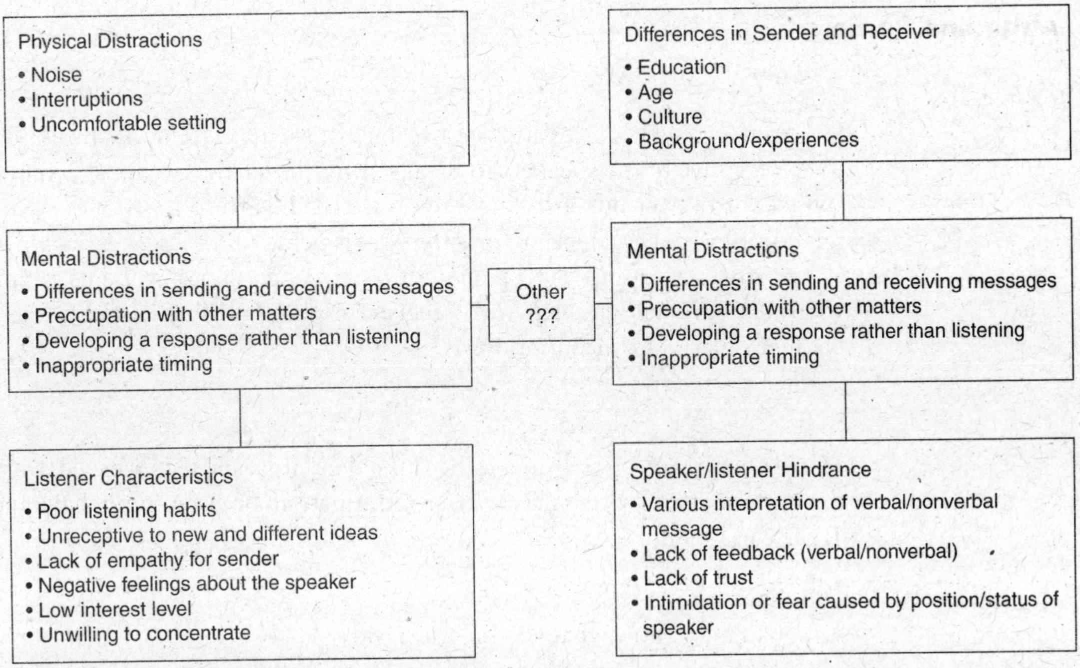

Figure 3.1 Barriers of effective listening.
Source: Adapted from William. C Himstreet, Wayne Murlin Baty and Caral M. Lehman. *Business Communications*, 10th edition (California: Wadsworth Publishing Company, 1993) 45.

Physiological Barriers

Speaking–Thinking Rate

According to an estimate, we speak at an average of 125–150 words a minute. Our mind, however, can process nearly 500 words per minute. This gives listeners a good deal of spare time, which is often used for mental excursions ranging from daydreaming to thinking about the speaker's hair-style. Spending this time for analysing the message would make for better listening.

Environmental Barriers

Physical Distractions

Distracting sounds, poor acoustics and uncomfortable seating arrangements can hamper effective listening.

Again, when you are forced to listen to a quick succession of messages, after a point, your receptivity dulls. You find it gets impossible to listen attentively.

Attitudinal Barriers

Prejudices

Sometimes our prejudices and deep-seated beliefs make it impossible for us to be receptive to the speaker. To break down this barrier, we must achieve some control over our instinctive responses and learn to postpone judgement until we have *listened* to exactly what is being said.

At times, we are preoccupied with other concerns. As students, all of you must have had days when you register nothing of what is said in class because of lack of concentration.

Egocentrism

Many people are poor listeners because they are overly concerned with themselves. Three personal concerns dominate their listening behaviour. These can be summed up in three sentences:

1. I must defend my position.
2. I already know what you have to say.
3. How am I coming through?

These concerns set up effective barriers that destroy the critical link between speaker and listener.

Poor Listening Habits

Listening, like much of human behaviour, tends to follow consistent patterns. Most of us develop certain bad listening habits that eventually create problems, as described in the following:

- **Faking attention:** For example, many of us fake attention so as not to appear discourteous. However, this can become habitual, and turn out to be a barrier to effective listening.
- **Listening only for facts:** In looking only for the facts, we often forget to locate the main idea.
- **Avoiding difficult and uninteresting material:** Sometimes we switch off our attention when what is being said is difficult, unfamiliar or simply uninteresting. If we do this often, this turning off becomes a consistent pattern.
- **Focusing on delivery:** Sometimes we are so concerned with how someone says something that we pay scant attention to what he or she is actually saying.

Lack of Common Experiences

It is difficult for a person to understand what is being said, if he or she has no experience, either direct or indirect, of the concepts being discussed.

APPROACHES TO LISTENING

Why do people listen at all? Sometimes people listen because they want some information from the speaker; sometimes they listen because they enjoy what they are hearing. Depending on the purpose, a listener adopts one of the following listening approaches discussed as follows.

Discriminative Listening

Discriminative listening involves an attempt to distinguish one sound from all the others. Stopping work to determine whether the phone is ringing is an example. We learn how to discriminate among sounds at an early age.

Comprehensive Listening

Comprehensive listening involves an attempt understand a speaker's message in totality and to interpret the meaning as precisely as possible. This kind of listening is generally practised in the classroom when we must remember what we have heard in a lecture and rely upon it for future use.

Critical Listening

When a person wants to sift through what he has heard and come to a decision, he must listen critically. This involves judging the clarity, accuracy and reliability of the evidence that is presented, and being alert to the effects of emotional appeals.

Active Listening

Active listening is also called empathies listening. This kind of listening goes beyond just paying attention or listening critically. It entails supportive behaviour that tells the speaker. *Understand Please go on.*

When you listen actively, you encourage the speaker to express himself fully. Sometimes active listeners provide the speakers with neutral summaries of what they have heard in order to affirm that they have understood what they have said. Active listening involves responding to the emotional content as well apart from the bare verbal message. An active listener is alert to all cues and carefully observes the nonverbal behaviour of the speaker to get the total picture.

HOW TO BE A BETTER LISTENER

Regardless of whether the situation calls for appreciative, critical, discriminative or active listening, listening skills can be improved with conscious effort. Table 3.1 shows the differences between good listeners and bad listeners. Let us now look at some of the specific steps you can take to become a better listener.

Be Motivated to Listen

When you resolve that you will listen, an improvement in your listening skills will become immediately noticeable. Researchers have concluded that the more motivated a listener is, the more active and alert he becomes as a receiver. Though motivation alone cannot solve all problems in listening, it is the first prerequisite to becoming a good listener.

Table 3.1 **Distinguishing good listeners from bad listeners**

To Listen Effectively	The Bad Listener	The Good Listener
1. Find areas of interest	Tunes out dry subjects	Opportunize; asks, 'what is in it for me?'
2. Judge content, not delivery	Tunes out if delivery is poor	Judges content; skips over delivery errors
3. Hold your fire	Tends to enter into Argument	Does not judge until comprehension is complete; interrupts only to clarity
4. Listen for ideas	Listens for facts	Listens for central themes
5. Be flexible	Takes extensive notes using only one system	Takes fewer notes; uses four to five different systems, depending on speaker
6. Work at listening	Shows no energy output; fakes attention	Works hard; exhibits active body state
7. Resist distractions	Is distracted easily	Fights or avoids distractions; tolerates bad habits; knows how to concentrate
8. Exercise your mind	Resists difficult expository material; seeks light, recreational material	Uses heavier material as exercise for the mind
9. Keep your mind open	Reacts to emotional words	Interprets emotional words; does not get hung up on them

Source: Adapted from C.L. Bovee and J.V. Thill, *Business Communication* (New York: McGraw, 1995) 571.

Be Prepared to Listen

Sometimes you need to make some preparation beforehand in order to listen effectively to a particular piece of communication. It is helpful to gather as much relevant information as you can about the subject, the speaker and the situation. This will help you to better understand and appraise what the speaker is saying. Preparations could also include attempts to minimize physical barriers between yourself and the speaker and to eliminate all distractions in the environment.

Be Objective

From your own experiences, you would have noticed that you are more receptive to a message when you approach it with an open mind.

Box 3.1: Are Men Listening?

Recent findings seem to confirm what women have suspected all along; men say they're listening, but they're really only giving it half their attention.

In fact they listen with the left side of their brain, while women use both the right and left sides, according to a study. But the authors of the study say this is not the time to resurrect gender stereotypes, and that the jury is still out on which sex really has the better listening skills.

'Language processing between men and women is different but it doesn't necessarily mean performance is different', says Michael Philips, assistant professor of radiology at Indiana University School of Medicine.

After playing a portion of the John Grisham novel, *The Partner*, to 20 men and 20 women for a period of less than 6 minutes, the researchers found that both had a similar grasp of the plot.

But what the magnetic resonance imaging (MRI) demonstrated was the markedly different ways they arrived at roughly the same point.

The MRI revealed that while brain activity in men was exclusively in the temporal lobe of the brain's left hemisphere, which is associated with listening and speech, the women also employed the right temporal lobe which is thought to help with performing music and understanding spatial relationships. 'It was a surprise result', says Philips.

HOW TO IMPROVE LISTENING SKILLS

The speaker, to a certain extent, influences the way in which others listen to the message. The speaker can use certain techniques to encourage more effective listening.

Try to Empathize

The best way to do improve listening skills is to imagine yourself in their position. This will help you to weed out uninteresting and difficult parts that may be irrelevant or could be made more easily understandable by being put in a different way.

Adjust Your Delivery

You can retain listeners' interest by modulating your voice and making your speech as lively as you can without sounding ridiculous.

Utilize Feedback

As the listener uses feedback to improve the communication, so can the speaker. Be sensitive to the listener's responses. Ask yourself: Are they paying attention? Do they look interested? Do they look confused? Are they bored? Answering these questions will help you to make the necessary adjustments and tailor your message to the needs of the audience.

Be Clear

Know your purpose. What is the main point that you are trying to make? If you are not clear about what you want to say and why you want to say it, you are likely to ramble aimlessly and it is very difficult to pay attention to disconnected and disjointed wanderings.

Be Interesting

Lack of interest on the speaker's part communicates itself immediately to the listeners and dulls their own response. Lively, stimulating and relevant speech always has a better chance of capturing the audience's attention.

THINK ABOUT IT

Most people spend at least half their communication time listening. This most-used communication skill is not only crucial in interpersonal communication, it also affects organizational communication and helps determine success in education and in careers. Business writer Kevin Murphy says, 'The better you listen, the luckier you will get'. So take time to listen.

4

Interpersonal Skills

In this chapter, we will discuss:

- Building Positive Relationships
- Giving Praise
- Dealing with Criticism
- Managing Conflict

In an organization, communication is largely about building team-oriented relationships marked by co-operation, honesty and mutual respect. After all, no man works alone in the workplace. He has to work with others. And his success in the workplace depends largely on how well he communicates with them and how well he works with them as a group .These skills, often referred to as 'people skills" or 'interpersonal skills', determine the quality of his relationships.

BUILDING POSITIVE RELATIONSHIPS

The ability to work well with others is no longer merely an additional asset for a manager. It is one of those vital abilities that sometimes makes the difference between success and failure. The quality of the personal relationships in an organization determines the communication culture of the firm. When people trust one another and believe that they are appreciated, the communication climate is a positive one. Psychologist Jack Gibb provides a list of ways to promote positive relationships.

Use Descriptive 'I' Language

Do not use a language that indicates accusation and threat. *Since you've been coming in late, I've had to make a lot of excuses whenever the Director asks for you. 'I' am uncomfortable with that*. Here too the speaker is pointing out someone that he is coming in late and that this is not acceptable. However, while the first sentence sounds judgemental, and is more likely to result in defensiveness, the second one is more descriptive. It has clear and specific statements and is not judgemental.

Focus on Solving Problems, Not Controlling Others

Controlling messages usually contain elements that attack the intelligence of the speaker. On the other hand, a problem-solving orientation focuses on identifying a problem that can be solved through mutual cooperation. Look at these two sentences.

1. *If you continue to come late to work I will have to sack you.*
2. *Let us try to figure out why you have difficulty coming to the office on time and see what we can do about it.*

The first sentence shows little regard for the other person's needs, while the second recognizes that there is a problem and suggests that it can be solved through joint effort.

Be Open: Do not Try to Deceive

Nobody likes to be manipulated or deceived. The moment somebody discovers that he has been tricked into a particular course of action through misleading or deceptive messages, he becomes extremely defensive. Being open in these circumstances is likely to generate less defensiveness. Even though others may not always like what you say, they will eventually grow to respect your intent.

Show Empathy

Lack of understanding interest of concern always creates defensiveness. Put yourself in the shoes of the secretary whose boss tells her:

'I don't care what your problems are; get this job done by the end of the day'.

Would not this kind of a message make you feel that you were being treated as an object rather than as a person with real feeling? When you empathize with your listener, you show concern for his opinions and assure him that he is valued. Now look at the same message rephrased '*I hope it will not be too difficult for you to complete this job today*'. While the first message conveys indifference, the second message shows greater sensitivity to the feeling and thoughts of the listener.

Do Not Put on an Air of Superiority

When you behave as though you are superior to the listener, you are implying that you have greater power, wealth, intelligence or social status. This encourages the listener to become defensive by ignoring or forgetting the message, or by establishing a competitive environment.

Listen with an Open Mind

It is always a good idea to hear out what others have to say with an open mind. A closed mind may imply to the other person that you do not care about the topic and that your mind is made up. For example, if the supervisor says, *'I have already seen two reports on why the plant should not be shifted, but may be your arguments will help us to look at the matter in a "different perspective"'*, you feel more comfortable, because you are sure the supervisor will at least give your ideas a fair hearing.

GIVING PRAISE

Praise, when used skilfully and when it is sincere, can go a long way towards establishing an enduring culture of motivation in an organization. Communication consultants Peter and Susan Glaser provide several tips on how to harness the power of praise.

Make Praise Specific

Although any kind of sincere praise is always welcome, praise becomes more meaningful when you spell out exactly what you appreciate. Telling your sales officer, *'you showed great ingenuity in dealing with that irate customer without losing your cool'*, tells him what exactly you appreciate about the way he handled the complaint.

Praise Progress, Not Just Perfection

Do not wait for a person to turn in an outstanding piece of work before you praise him. Chances are, you may never get a chance to do so. Instead, focus on the progress the person makes. You can always motivate a person to try harder by complimenting any improvement in his performance.

Be Sincere

Praise that is not sincere can be highly counterproductive. In the words of Bob Nelson, founder of Nelson Motivation Inc.:

Do Not Overdo Praise

Like all other good things, 'praise' too can become inefficient if it is overdone. Constant praise becomes meaningless, as it sounds insincere.

Get the Timing Right

Praise given as soon as an achievement is complete, or the desired behaviour is displayed, is always more effective.

DEALING WITH CRITICISM

While praise is always a pleasure to give and receive, there are situations where you must grapple with something not quite so pleasant—criticism. Sometimes you have to make a critical remark about somebody, and sometimes you may be at the receiving end. By managing criticism well, both as the critic and as the criticized, you can avoid conflict and maintain good working relationships.

Offering Constructive Criticism

As a critic, you can ensure that your comments meet with the least resistance by taking care of some of these aspects.

- **Understand why you are making a critical remark.** Be sure that your criticism is appropriate to the situation and constructive for the parties involved. Criticizing somebody out of self-interest or envy may prove destructive.

- **Try to understand the other person's perspective.** Putting yourself in the other man's shoes will always help you to deal with the situation better.

- **Direct criticism at the person's behaviour, not at the person.** Your criticism should be focused on something that the person did or did not do, not on his 'traits' or 'character' in general. Be specific about what you are criticizing; deal with who, what, where and when.

- **Avoid sounding judgemental.** Even though criticism implies evaluation, emphasize description by using 'I' language, as described earlier. Avoid using provocative language.

- **Do not force criticism on anyone.** Present criticism in such a way as to encourage the other person to make decisions. People are more likely to comply with solutions they have generated themselves.

- **Avoid critical overload.** If you make several complaints at one time, there is every likelihood that the other person may go on the defensive and stop being receptive.

Responding to Criticism

Responding to criticism without resorting to either 'fight' or 'flight' takes a lot of skill. Some of the following guidelines can be of help:

- Recognize the value of constructive criticism. Such criticism can improve relationships and productivity.
- Try to understand the perspective of the person offering the criticism.
- Acknowledge criticism that focuses on your behaviour. Try to transform criticism that seems directed at your 'person' to specific acts or behaviour.
- Try to understand accurately the criticism being offered. You can do this by paraphrasing what the other person is saying, asking questions and checking out nonverbal cues.
- Maintain your authority to make your own decisions. Do not let a 'personal' attack weaken your resolve. Focus the other person's criticism on specific action and assert your right to generate solutions.
- Seek constructive changes to the behaviour that prompted the criticism.
- Communicate clearly how you feel and what you think about the criticism. Use 'I' messages.

MANAGING CONFLICT

Conflicts are inevitable. However, a great deal depends on how the conflict is handled. While unmanaged or badly managed conflict damages relationships, managed conflicts can lead to creative solutions, greater job satisfaction and better relationships.

Approaches to Conflict

When faced with a conflict, different people respond in different ways. Let us look at some of these approaches.

Avoiding

Unwillingness to talk things out, pretending that a conflict does not exist, making attempts to smooth things over when differences appear are all characteristic of this approach.

Accommodating

While avoiders shut themselves out, accommodators neglect their own concerns in order to satisfy the concerns of others. They are usually more concerned with being liked and getting along than with being right.

Competing

A person who adopts this approach is committed to his own position or perspective and considers relationships as secondary issues. Though this approach does generate ill will, it is costly and unpleasant.

Collaborating

This approach focuses on satisfying both parties to the greatest degree. It is a cooperative nature. Both parties work together to resolve conflicts in a way that meets the concerns of both. While a collaborative style is neither a panacea nor appropriate in all cases, it is particularly effective.

Compromising

Though this approach is also cooperative in nature, the cooperation here is dictated by self-interest. Each party forgoes something that it is seeking in order to reach an agreement. Here the goal is an expedient, mutually acceptable solution that partially satisfies both.

Resolving Conflict

Communication skills are at the heart of conflict management. Ultimately, it is the way you present your ideas and feelings that makes for either rancour and animosity or receptiveness and a sense of cooperation. It is alright to express feelings of hurt, anger, disappointment or disgust. But you can always do that without blaming somebody else for the way you feel. Perhaps you could offer alternative information or performance suggestions in a non-accusatory manner. For instance, instead of shouting at *your subordinate and saying, 'you idiot, you blew it'*, it would be a better idea if you gave the matter some more thought and said something like, '*Since this approach has not really worked well, perhaps we should adopt the consumer durable section's sales promotion drive*'. Avoiding emotional words that trigger a negative response is crucial. Perhaps one of the best kinds of awareness is knowing when to keep quiet. Following are a few strategies for defusing and redefining a conflict:

- **Restate:** Make sure everyone hears the same message.
- **Agree:** Focus on areas of agreement.

- **Refocus:** Try to see the 'big picture' instead of trivialities.
- **Dissect:** Separate the main issue from personal feelings.
- **Compliment:** Acknowledge the merits of the other person.
- **Compromise:** Settle for less than 100 per cent.
- **Postpone:** Allow for cool-down time before resolution.
- **Exit:** Leave the scene before you become angry.

THINK ABOUT IT

In today's business world, good interpersonal skills are essential for success. No individual, no matter how brilliant or talented, can hope to make it to the more coveted posts and stay there if he cannot work harmoniously with a group of people. Not only individual success, even the success of the organization as a whole depends to a great extent on whether the workforce has the necessary 'interpersonal skills' to establish a positive work environment.

5

Negotiations

In this chapter, we will discuss:

- Approaches to Negotiation
- The Major Elements of Negotiation Preparation
- The Situation

APPROACHES TO NEGOTIATION

As with conflict management, negotiation can be handled in different ways. The outcome of a negotiation depends on the approach.

Bargaining Orientation

This approach is based on the premise that one person can win only at the expense of the other —that any victory by one party must be matched by the other's loss. That is why this is also called the win–lose approach. This is sometimes the best approach when the other party is determined to take advantage of you or when your interests truly conflict with those of the other party and compromising is not a satisfactory option.

Lose–Lose Orientation

This is adopted when one negotiation partner feels his own interests are threatened and reacts by doing all he can to ensure that the outcome of the negotiation does not serve the other party's interests either. In effect, everybody ends up being a loser. Lose–lose outcomes occur when negotiating partners ignore one another's needs or when the need to hurt each other outweighs the need to find some kind of an acceptable solution.

Compromise

A compromise is the best way out when it is impossible for both parties to convince each other or when even the partial attainment of one party's goals depends on the satisfaction of the other. Compromise is a good option when disputed resources are limited. For instance, if two managers each need a full-time secretary, but budget restrictions make this impossible, they may have to compromise by sharing one secretary.

Win–Win Orientation

When the needs of the negotiating parties are compatible, it is a win–win solution. Its approach is superior to other problem-solving styles, because everyone ends up feeling satisfied. This approach works well when the following steps are adhered to:

- **Determine the needs of both parties.** If both parties can identify what issues are important to the other, they would find it easier to work towards a mutually acceptable solution.
- **Develop a list of possible solutions.** Once the basic issues have been identified, the two parties can sit together and come up with several solutions that would satisfy everyone's needs. All possible solutions are put down, without any of them being evaluated.
- **Choose the most appropriate solutions.** At this stage, each solution is evaluated and the ones that are most promising are adopted.
- **Implement the solution.** Once the best solution is decided upon, make sure everyone understands it, and then implement it.
- **Follow up on the solution.** Even the best plans need to be monitored after they have been implemented. A while after the plan has been put into action, meet with the other parties involved and discuss how the solution is working out. If anyone's needs are still unmet, you could go back to the problem-solving procedure and identify another solution.

THE MAJOR ELEMENTS OF NEGOTIATION PREPARATION

Success in negotiation is possible if you are well prepared and confident as it can always give you an edge in any communication process.

Understand the People Involved

Note that it is important to know something about the people with whom we must negotiate and the organization they represent. What are their roles, their objectives? What problems will they raise? Are they in a position to make a difference or will they have to consult someone else? The answers to these questions will help you to better handle the issues that come up during the actual negotiation.

Know Your Objectives

Having your objectives clearly in mind is very important. Before negotiating identify the objectives, decide what the priorities are, what the variables are and what should be your attitude to each. To be well prepared, you must know exactly how much you are willing to concede or compromise on each factor. You must also have ready all the arguments you may need to justify your point of view, particularly on those points which you want to win.

Conduct

Two factors that operate during the actual negotiation are the tactics of negotiation and the interpersonal behaviour that accompanies them.

- **Aim high.** For example, it pays off to aim for the best deal you can imagine. You can always trade down. If you start too low, it is difficult to trade up, particularly at a late stage in the process.
- **Get the other person's shopping list.** Also it is important to identify what the other party wants, and what he is likely to concede. This will help you to assess the situation better.
- **Keep the whole package in mind.** Focus on the total situation—your views and the other party's—so that you proceed conscious of everything (or as much as possible) that will be involved.
- **Keep searching for variables.** Remain flexible. What you plan beforehand should never act like a straightjacket. Sometimes matters proceed along the lines you expect; many times they do not. Adapting and fine-tuning may always be required.

When the negotiation starts the two parties are at opposite ends of the scale. However, by the time the negotiation closes, they are expected to settle on something they can both relate to as a 'good deal'.

Sometimes the first round of negotiation only serves to induce both parties to shift to a more reasonable initial stance.

As negotiation is essentially a communication process; its success, to a great extent, will depend on how well the two parties can build what are called 'bridges to rapport'. These bridges help them to see each other's point of view and to relate to each other.

Overall, success in negotiation comes largely from good listening skills, the ability to communicate persuasively and good interpersonal skills. Negotiations will not produce the desired effect unless those involved consciously address both the solid facts and the human dimension.

6

Interviewing

In this chapter, we will discuss:

- Planning Interviews
- Conducting Interviews
- The Ethics of Interviewing

An interview is a goal-oriented, interpersonal communication between an interviewer and a respondent. It is primarily undertaken to accomplish a specific purpose, perhaps to obtain or provide information, to solve a problem or to persuade someone to undertake some action. The style and structure of an interview depends on its purpose and on the relationship between the two parties involved. Following are different types of business interviews.

Employment Interviews

Employment interviews provide general information to potential applicants before a vacancy arises, or take place when a specific job opening is available and applicants are to be screened for the position. Ultimately, the employment interview seeks to determine whether a particular applicant is suitable for the job.

Performance Appraisal Interviews

Performance appraisal interviews provide job-related feedback to employees. A supervisor and an employee together assess how much progress the employee has made towards the achievement of certain predetermined goals.

Counselling Interviews

Counselling interviews provide guidance and assistance to employees. Such interviews sometimes involve very personal and emotional issues, such as family problems, drinking or drugs, that affect the employee's performance.

Disciplinary Interviews

Disciplinary interviews become necessary when there are disruptive problems that must be curtailed. Some of the most common problems that warrant disciplinary action are nonperformance of duties, chronic absenteeism, disobedience or insubordination and damaging of property.

Persuasive Interviews

Persuasive interviews, which primarily seek to induce somebody to adopt a new idea, product or service, are generally associated with selling. To conduct a successful persuasive interview, the interviewer has to use all his communication skills, draw out opinions of the respondent and to impart information.

PLANNING THE INTERVIEW

Whatever the type of interview, a good deal of planning is necessary to make the interview a success. There are six strategies for planning an interview—state the purpose, get information about the other party, decide the structure, consider possible questions, plan the physical setting and anticipate problems.

State the Purpose

As an interview is a communication process it must have a specific goal, so that the structure of the interview and the actual questions can be tailored to suit that particular purpose. On the respondent's part, lack of a clear purpose can cause him to send out conflicting signals which often undermine his chances of achieving his goal.

Get Information About the Other Party

In order to make the best case for your candidacy for a particular job, you need to be prepared with information about yourself and about the job, the company and the field.

The interviewer too finds it easier to restrict himself to relevant questions if he is familiar with the details the applicant has provided in his application form or resume.

Decide the Structure

Interviews can be structured in different ways. The structure determines what kind of planning you ought to put in and what sort of results you can expect.

In a directive interview, the interviewer takes almost complete charge of the flow of conversation by asking specific questions designed to keep the respondent focused on the type of information required. Such questions are called close-ended questions, as they seek to elicit precise information on a specific issue. A directive approach is useful when you are looking for precise, reliable information in a short time. However, a directive approach limits the respondent's initiative and may prevent him from volunteering useful information. When you want to not only obtain factual information but also gauge the underlying feelings of the respondent or draw out his opinions on different issues, a nondirective approach works better. This approach, with its open-ended questions, gives the respondent more control in determining the course of the interview. The interviewer does a minimum of talking and encourages the respondent to fully express his feelings. In an actual interview, most questions fall along a continuum of openness. As an interviewer, you can frame questions towards any one end of the spectrum, depending on the purpose you want to achieve.

Consider Possible Questions

Factual questions seek to ascertain facts, while opinion questions ask for the respondent's judgements. Primary questions introduce new topics or new areas within a topic and secondary questions seek additional information on a topic that has already been introduced. Direct and indirect questions are two different ways of eliciting information. Though direct questions are usually the best way to get information, sometimes they fail to elicit satisfactory answers, either because the respondent is unable to answer accurately or is unwilling to do so.

Direct Questions

Do you understand?
Are you satisfied with my leadership?

Indirect Questions

If you had to explain this policy to a newcomer, what would you say?
If you were made the manager of this department, what changes would you make?

You may also decide to include hypothetical and leading questions. Hypothetical questions are 'what if' questions: If I were to introduce flexible working hours, do you think the morale of the staff would improve? These questions can indirectly get a respondent to describe his attitudes. They also let you learn how a person would behave in certain situations. Leading questions force the respondent to answer in a particular way, by suggesting the answer the interviewer expects such as: *You would not mind working extra hours whenever necessary, would you?*

CONDUCTING INTERVIEWS

The Opening

The opening is usually used to put the respondent at ease and to establish the purpose of the interview. To put the respondent at ease, the interviewer usually follows the initial greeting with a brief informal conversation, helping the respondent to relax and builds a rapport with him. Whatever the nature of the interview, the outcomes are likely to be better when the interviewer and the respondent are comfortable with each other.

Body

The Interviewer's Role

It is the interviewer's responsibility to control and focus the conversation so that the discussion does not drift away from the agenda. The interviewer also has to ensure that he allots enough time to each item of the agenda. If he lingers too long on one topic, he may not have enough time to do justice to other areas that are equally important.

Interviewers must listen actively in order to pick up verbal and nonverbal cues. Sometimes they are so caught up in framing their own questions and responses that they fail to hear what the respondent is actually saying. An alert interviewer must not only pay attention to the respondent's verbal messages, but pick up nonverbal signals too, that may provide insights into the respondent's behaviour and attitudes.

Skilful use of probing questions will improve the results. Sometimes the interviewer can effectively use silence to induce the respondent to volunteer more details or a more satisfactory explanation. Summarizing the main points from time to time will also helps to ensure that the interviewer and the respondent have the same understanding.

The Respondent's Role

The respondent can take several proactive steps to ensure that he makes a favourable impression. The most important of these is to answer all questions as clearly and accurately as possible. A respondent who fails to give clear answers is either seen as having failed to understand the question or as wanting to evade the issue.

Sometimes interviewers misinterpret facts. When this happens, it is up to the respondent to ensure that the record is set straight. He can do this by politely pointing out that he had said something else, or by unobtrusively repeating an earlier remark, so that the misunderstanding is cleared. The respondent should also make sure that his answers are all tailored to achieving his purpose in attending the interview. The answers should be honest, but must always focus on the positive aspects.

Closing

Once the last question has been asked and answered, the interview can be rounded by a restatement of conclusions. This signals that you have finished and gives the respondent an opportunity to ask relevant questions. The interviewer then gives the respondent some idea of what future action he can expect before concluding with pleasantries.

THE ETHICS OF INTERVIEWING

Communication between the interviewer and the respondent should be guided by certain ethical guidelines. This paves the way for better interactions in future. They are as follows:

Guidelines for the Interviewer

Do not make unrealistic promises.
Do not reveal confidential information.
Do not ask illegal questions.
Do not be controlling or overbearing.
Do not be overly friendly.

Guidelines for the Respondent

Do not be dishonest.
Do not waste the interviewer's time.

7

Group Communication

In this chapter, we will discuss:

- Factors in Group Communication
- Group Decision-making
- Effective Meetings

Communication among the members of a group leads to group decisions. If these decisions are to be effective, every member of the group must be able to communicate freely and openly with all the other members of the group. Groups generally develop certain norms about discussion and group members develop roles that affect the group's interaction.

FACTORS IN GROUP COMMUNICATION

There are several factors that affect the group dynamics and thereby shape the outcome of the group discussions. Let us consider a few of these (Table 7.1).

Leadership

Leadership that aims at achieving task goals, while at the same time maintaining interpersonal relationships in the group, is likely to make for greater group success.

Status

Sometimes some members of a group have a better social standing or are better qualified than the others. The status of the members determines the manner in which they interact with each other. People tend to communicate with peers as their equals, but they tend to speak upward to their superiors and downward to their subordinates.

Table 7.1 Roles People Play in Groups

Self-oriented Roles	Group Maintenance Roles	Task-facilitating Roles
Controlling: Dominating others by exhibiting superiority or authority. **Withdrawing:** Retiring from the group either by becoming silent or by refusing to deal with a particular aspect of the group's work. **Attention seeking:** Calling attention to oneself and demanding recognition from others. **Diverting:** Focusing group discussion on topics of interest to the individual rather than those relevant to the task.	**Encouraging:** Drawing out other members by showing verbal and nonverbal support, praise or agreement. **Harmonizing:** Reconciling differences among group members through mediation or by using humour to relieve tension. **Compromising:** Offering to yield on a point in the interest of reaching a mutually acceptable decision.	**Initiating:** Getting the group started on a line of inquiry. **Information giving or seeking:** Offering (or seeking) information relevant to questions facing the group **Coordinating:** Showing relationships among ideas, clarifying issues, summarizing what the group has done. **Procedure setting:** Suggesting decision-making procedures that will move the group towards a goal.

Source: C.L. Bovee and J.V. Thill. *Business Communication Today* (New York: McGraw Hill 1995).

Brainstorming

Sometimes brainstorming sessions are used to arrive at a decision. Members are encouraged to generate as many ideas about a topic as they can. Every idea is recorded. No idea is rejected at the initial stage. The group then returns to the ideas and adopts those that seem most feasible or most useful.

Nominal Group Technique

Nominal group technique is a decision-making tool that is used when the group must rank a see options. Members individually list all options that can be considered. The group facilitator then asks each member to rank all the options from the lowest to the highest in priority. The facilitator then computes an average score for each idea to determine the group's highest priority.

The Final Decision

There are many ways that a group can make a final decision, agree on a solution and come to an agreement. Some of the popular ways of making decisions include the following:

- **Consensus:** All the group members agree on the final decision after discussion to debate.
- **Compromise:** Group members come to an agreement by giving up some of the demands.

- **Majority vote:** The decision is based on the opinion of the majority of its members.
- **Decision by leader:** The group allows its leader to take the final decision.
- **Arbitration:** An external body or person makes a decision for the group.

Now that we have looked at some of the aspects of group dynamics, let us take a closer look at the actual interaction between group members when they get together to discuss common concerns, in other words, when they get together for a meeting.

EFFECTIVE MEETINGS

The success of a meeting depends on the ability of each individual member of a group to communicate with the rest of the group as a whole. Over the years, the 'meeting' in many organizations has come to be associated with wasted time and boredom. There are several reasons for failure of meetings. One is that they are held at regular intervals for no particular reason. Sometimes there are too many people present to make an effective decision. To set the stage for a successful meeting, careful planning is crucial.

The Planning Process

To plan a meeting the convener must consider the following important questions:

- Why have a meeting at all?
- What is the purpose of the meeting?
- Who should be asked to participate?
- Where should the meeting be held?
- When should it be held?

Why Have a Meeting at All?

This question underlines the need for a specific purpose. Some meetings have a long-standing purpose. For instance, the daily morning briefings in police stations in which officers are briefed about the recent developments before they begin their patrol. Meetings that do not have any such ongoing purpose need to have their true purpose defined clearly. For instance, a meeting called to present the company's alternative home loan scheme may have either of these three purposes: to inform the employees about the alternatives so that they can choose the one they want to allow the group to decide, whether they want to adopt the new plan, or to persuade employees to opt for the new plan.

Informational meetings: These are the easiest to plan. The purpose is to inform the group about recent developments. The convener does most of the talking but there is also scope for two-way communication. This enables the convener to get feedback from the group about whether they understand and accept the new proposals.

Problem-solving meetings: These meetings usually have fewer participants than informational meetings. Problem-solving meetings usually focus on arriving at a decision—changing existing procedures, adopting a new system, etc. Sometimes such meetings are also used to generate new ideas.

Who Should Participate?

The answer to this question depends on the purpose for which the meeting is held. If the meeting is informational, a large number of people may be invited. If the meeting is called to take a decision, fewer people should be invited, so that all can participate in the discussion. In this case, the convener should invite only those who have expertise in the area and those who have the authority to make a decision.

Where Should the Meeting be Held?

The 'where' of a meeting is usually decided by custom or availability of space. The seating arrangements can have a bearing on the final outcome of the meeting. Figure 7.1 shows a number of seating arrangements. The theatre style and the classroom style are appropriate for large groups that are meeting to obtain information. The leader does much of the talking and participation is limited. The banquet style allows members to see each other and the 'T' formation brings participants closer together, but the focus is still on the leaders. These arrangements can be used for meetings designed to facilitate change. Problem-solving meetings generally have the conference table seating arrangements. How far individual members are expected to participate in the meeting depends on how the leader positions himself in relation to the other participants. The conveners must also consider the timing of the meeting.

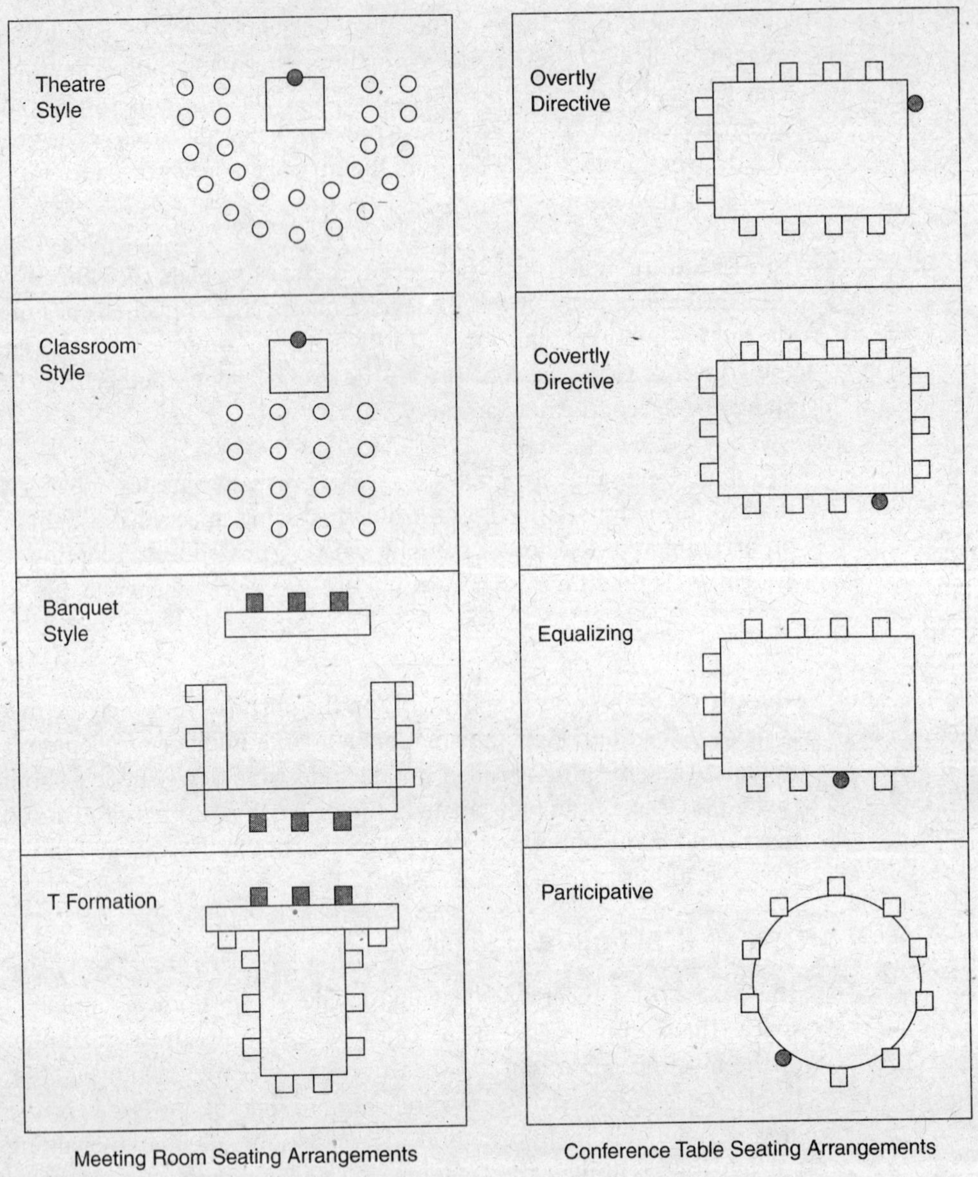

Figure 7.1 Meeting room seating arrangements.
Soruce: Gibson and Hodgetls. *Business Communication* (New York: Harper and Row, 1990).

When Should the Meeting Be Held?

In deciding when the meeting should be held, the convener should consider the schedules of the participants. Early Monday morning is seldom a good time for a meeting as most participants are anxious to get on with their week's schedule. Similarly, meetings scheduled for the afternoon of the last day of the week—Friday or Saturday—draw a poor response as most participants are preoccupied with their plans for the weekend.

Notice

Once these questions have been considered, the convener of the meeting must issue a notice. A notice should have the following:

- Be issued by the proper authority
- Observe a minimum period of notice
- State where and when the meeting is to be held
- Be accompanied by an agenda
- Be sent to all individuals entitled to receive it

Agenda

The notice, as mentioned earlier, must be accompanied by an agenda. An agenda is a list of topics that will be covered at the meeting. Agenda gives the participants a chance to gather their thoughts and bring relevant information to the meeting.

To be effective, an agenda must be specific. The topics listed should not be vague. They must spell out what exactly will be discussed. Any relevant background reading material should be attached. The list of topics to be taken up for discussion should not be too long. Meetings that go on and on are not very popular.

Minutes

The minutes of the previous meeting are sometimes circulated along with the agenda. The recipients are supposed to read them before attending the meeting. If the minute is not sent along with the agenda, it is read out by the secretary when the meeting starts. This is generally a brief, accurate record of the business transacted at the previous meeting. It should contain the following:

- Name of the organization
- Place, date and time of meeting
- Names of the chairperson and secretary
- Names of other members present
- All motions and amendments
- Names of the movers and seconders of all motions and amendments
- Results of the voting

The minutes should be as follows:

- Concise but sufficiently detailed to make clear what the meeting was about
- Precise and unambiguous
- Impersonal and impartial
- Written in the past tense
- Numbered in ascending order from one meeting to another

Conducting Business

In order to accomplish the desired objectives of the meeting, the leader must follow the agenda. Whenever the discussion strays from the agenda, he should redirect it, so that it stays focused on the main purpose.
Not all ideas that come up during a meeting may be relevant or practicable. When someone comes up with an irrelevant or unsuitable idea, the leader may suggest that it may be taken up at some other time when it would be more appropriate. The leader should thank the people for their participation, regardless of how he personally feels about their ideas.

Concluding the Meeting

A little before the scheduled closing time, the leader usually signals that time is almost up. This gives the group a chance to wrap up the discussion. He then brings the meeting to a close by noting what has been accomplished and what remains to be done. Participants should be informed about what will happen next. If decisions have been made and action promised, the group members should be told when the action will be taken. Members should also be informed about when the minutes of the meeting will be circulated.

THINK ABOUT IT

Careful planning and skillful leadership make for effective meetings, without which meetings are bound to be looked upon as a waste of time, effort and financial resources. They may seem to lack focus and appear to be unproductive. However, group meetings can be a great asset if they are planned properly and administered effectively.

8

Making Presentations—Getting Started

In this chapter, we will discuss:

- Speech Purposes—General
- Speech Purposes—Specific
- Methods of Speaking
- Analysing the Audience
- Nonverbal Dimensions of Presentation

Most communication acts are initiated because individual seeks to accomplish a purpose or fulfil a goal. In public speaking, which is simply a specialized form of communication, the speaker wants a specific response from the audience and communicates in order to secure that response. Hence, the speaker has a preconceived purpose that has been decided upon before the talk begins. In facts, to be a successful speaker you must determine and clarify your purpose before you send your message. By deciding upon the response you want from your audience, you can better select the ideas, the organizational patterns, the language and the delivery methods that will enable you to reach your goal. Salespersons' ultimate purpose is to persuade.

There are three general speech purposes—to inform, to persuade and to entertain. (These three purposes apply equally to public or private communication.)

Informative Speeches

The purpose of informative communication is to increase the receiver's knowledge and understanding of a subject. Informative speeches may also entertain or change beliefs. A speaker whose immediate purpose is to impart information often uses amusing dramatic illustrations to entertain his or her audience, thus holding their attention. Moreover, information, even if it consists only of facts, may lead to changes of behaviour, although such results may not be a part of the speaker's purpose.

In informative speaking, the main concern of the speaker is to make the audience understand and remember the information presented. The teacher talking to a class or the manager of a department store explaining the duties of a job to staff members are both engaged in informative speaking. How much the listener understands at the end of the speech is the real test of the speaker.

Some examples of informative subjects are as follows:

- How to grow vegetables in a greenhouse.
- The working of a pollution-free engine.

Persuasive Speeches

The major objective of the persuasive speech is to induce the audience to think, feel and act in a manner intended by the speaker. For example, the salesperson uses his speech as a means to persuade a customer to buy a coat. The person asking for a raise, the wife trying to get her husband to fix the tap, the teacher trying to get the class to study—all are trying to persuade someone to do something.

The following are examples of subjects that need persuasive treatment:

- Final examinations in our colleges should be abolished.
- Students should be given time off to campaign on behalf of political candidates.

Entertaining Speeches

The third major type of speech is the purpose of entertaining the audience, that is, stimulating pleasurable response, whether it be humorous or dramatic.

Through such speeches, the speaker wants the audience to have an enjoyable time. Here the speaker is not concerned about ensuring that they learn a great deal or that they change their mind in one direction or another. Entertainment is the purpose of many after-dinner speeches and the favourite type of speech of comedians.

Some of the subjects that lead themselves to humorous treatment are as follows:

- My first day as a college student.
- How to write a political speech.

SPEECH PURPOSE—SPECIFIC

Specific purpose speech describes the exact nature of the response you want from your audience. It states specifically what you want your audience to know, feel, believe or do.

There are three requirements a good specific purpose should meet: it should contain only one central idea; it should be clear and concise; and, most important, it should be worded in terms of the desired audience response.

If your general purpose is to persuade, your specific purpose might be the following:

- To get the audience to give money to a college fund to beautify the campus.
- To get the audience to agree that India should withdraw all its soldiers from Kashmir.
- To get the audience to agree that we should have a department of women's studies at our university.

METHODS OF SPEAKING

Regardless of your background, knowledge or skill, each time you speak it is a different and unique experience. Effective communicators recognize these differences and prepare specifically for each particular occasion. Included in their thought preparation will be an analysis of the type of delivery best suited for their subject, audience and occasion.

There are four fundamental ways of presenting a speech:

1. reading from manuscript
2. speaking from memory
3. delivering in an impromptu manner and
4. speaking extemporaneously. Bear in mind that there are many speaking situations that call for a combination of two or three of these types.

Speaking from a manuscript is a form of delivery where you read your speech directly from a manuscript. For example, this form is common in radio and television speeches. At conventions and business meetings manuscript is helpful for the speaker who would like his speech to be circulated.

An obvious advantage of this method is that it puts no strain on the speaker's memory. Another advantage is that the manuscript, having been written well in advance of the speech situation, enables the speaker to be very selective and meticulous in his style and choice of materials.

However, there are also serious disadvantages to this type of delivery. One main disadvantage is that the speaker often loses sight of the importance of communication. You repeat your remarks and many times fail to establish a rapport with your listeners as the manuscript becomes more significant than the audience, and all sense of spontaneity is forgotten.

Speaking from Memory

The memorized speech, much like the manuscript, allows the speaker the advantage of carefully worked out and worded speech. Every single word is committed to the speaker's memory and this, of course, frees him from the manuscript.

Impromptu Delivery

When you are asked to speak on the spur of the moment, without advance notice time on a specific topic, you are engaging in impromptu speaking. It has been remarked that much of our conversation is nothing more than a series of impromptu talks.

Extemporaneous Delivery

The extemporaneous delivery is often referred to as the 'middle course'. This particular speech form is by far the most desirable of the four.

Extemporaneous speaking calls for the speech to be (i) researched (ii) outlined (iii) practised and (iv) delivered in a conversational manner. Because you know about the speaking assignment beforehand, you have time to conduct research and gather necessary information.

Once the data is gathered, the extemporaneous speaker must organize and outline the material into a clear and systematic pattern. A major advantage of the extemporaneous speech is that it is prepared in advance, and is therefore well organized.

ANALYSING THE AUDIENCE

To communicate your purpose effectively, you need to understand the audience. Audience analysis means, in a very practical sense, finding out all you can about the people you are talking to or will be talking to. You discover what your receivers are like so that you can adapt your material directly to their needs, wants, experiences and attitudes. Only by seeing things from their viewpoint can you deal directly with their predispositions. Remember that communication is a two-way process involving sender and receiver, and that the heart of communication is the behaviour change. In order to change people's behaviour, we must deal directly with them.

As a public speaker, you must also make an analysis of your audience if your speech is to be meaningful. The speaker who presents a speech without considering the audience has very little chance of gaining support or being understood. Audience analysis enables you to establish a rapport with your listeners. By understanding your audience, you can adapt your materials—and yourself—to the people with whom you want to communicate.

To predict possible audience responses, it is crucial to understand the following information:

- The age of your listeners.
- The sex of your listeners.
- The occupation of your listeners.
- Intelligence and educational level of your listeners.
- The social, professional and religious groups your listeners belong to.
- The influence of geographical locations.

In addition to exploring the backgrounds of your listeners, you will find a number of other useful questions once you have established a profile of your audience.

The answer to each of these questions will enable the speaker to understand the entire speaking situation. Once you are able to see and feel as the audience does, you are in a position to put into words those ideas that will elicit maximum agreement and understanding.

To be an effective speaker, the verbal and nonverbal elements of the presentation have to be aligned so as to convey the same message and thus, support each other. How can you ensure this alignment of the verbal and nonverbal elements of oral presentation? One way, of course, is by reading about them. By gaining an awareness of the role each nonverbal element plays in influencing listener reaction to the verbal message you may learn how to make constructive use of these elements and avoid placing banners it your path to communication effectiveness.

THINK ABOUT IT

Since communication is normally intended to convey a specific message, speakers must be clear about the purpose of their presentation. This 'purpose' must be reflected in their selection and organization of material for the speech. The nonverbal elements of the presentation must also convey this message for effective communication to take place.

Speeches can be broadly divided into three purposes: to inform, to persuade and to entertain. To formulate a more specific purpose, the speaker must determine exactly what kind of response he wants from the audience. And to convey this purpose effectively, it must be adapted to the audience's needs. In order to do this, the speaker should analyse the audience. Valuable insight into the listeners' needs, wants, attitudes and experiences can be gained by discovering their age, sex, occupation, intelligence and education, and social, professional and religious affiliations, and geographical experiences.

Armed with a knowledge of the audience, a clear sense of purpose, and an awareness of the power of nonverbal elements, the speaker should select his material, organize it and practise his speech. Speakers are not just 'born'; with practice, they can be 'made'.

9

Communication for Employment—Application Letter

In this chapter, we will discuss:

- Qualities of Well-written Application Letters
- Letter Plan

You have indentified the position for which you would like to apply. You have prepared an effective resumé. The next step is to write a letter of application. Like the resumé, the application letter is also a tool to sell yourself. To use this tool effectively, focus on what you can do for your prospective employer and why you believe you are well qualified for the position. Your letter must arouse the employer's interest in your resumé and improve your chances of being granted an interview. The more effectively you consider the employer's perspective, the more attention your letter will receive. Tailor your letter to the unique requirements of the position for which you are applying, the company to which you are applying and the industry to which the job belongs.

When you send an application letter to a company in response to an advertisement of an opening, or upon learning about an opening from some other source, such an application is a solicited letter of application. When you send a letter without knowing whether an opening actually exists, you are sending an unsolicited application letter. This must have more powerful attention-getters than a solicited letter.

If a resumé is sent along with the letter, as is generally the case, the letter does not have to be as thorough as the letter sent without a resumé. A letter accompanying a resumé is a supplement to, rather than a substitute for, the resumé.

QUALITIES OF WELL-WRITTEN APPLICATION LETTERS

The You-attitude

One of the most important qualities of a well-written application letter is the use of the you-attitude. In other words, focus on the reader and his needs rather than on your own wishes.

Consider these two opening sentences:

1. *I wish to be considered an applicant for the position of sales representative.*
2. *A degree in marketing and my interpersonal skills would enable me to be the 'enthusiastic, hard-working sales representative' you advertised for in the Economic Times dated 12 October.* Which of these two openings do you think is more effective? Why?

Length

The length of an application is another important quality. It is best to limit the application letter to one page, and to four or five paragraphs, unless a longer letter is absolutely essential. Of course, you must provide all relevant information that is likely to rouse the reader's interest and help him see how your services would benefit the organization.

Addressed to A Person Not to A Title

Whenever possible address your letter to a person not to a title. It is worthwhile to spend some time and effort to learn the name of the person to whom you are sending the letter. After all, a letter addressed to 'Mr. Gagan Bhujbal' does create a more favourable impression than one addressed to the 'Human Resources Manager', provided, of course, that you have not misspelt the manager's name.

Knowledge of Employer's Activities

The company to which you are applying may have recently acquired another company or introduced a new product. Sentences that imply your knowledge of these developments are likely to make a favourable impression. They show that you are really interested in the field, that you gathered information before making decisions and so on.

Knowledge of Job Requirements

You need not have to repeat the job requirements. The employer already knows them. But if a particular job lays emphasis on certain skills, then you could always provide information that shows your awareness of the emphasis without stating it directly. For example, a marketing job requires frequently travelling. Instead of writing, 'I understand the job requires frequent travelling', you could refer to other work experience that required you to travel a lot or your preference for work that requires travelling.

Reader-benefit Information

A well-written application letter usually contains reader-benefit material, explaining what you can do for the reader. Your education and trainings and/or personal traits usually constitute the main reasons the employer will recruit you. It is for you to ensure that you convert factual information of this nature into material that the reader can use to his advantage.

Organization

Like the sales letter, the application letter focuses on a central selling point. This is introduced in the first or the second paragraph and stressed in the paragraphs that follow. Reference to the enclosed resumé is best included at the end of the middle section of the letter. Putting it earlier may prompt the reader to put the letter aside and look at the resumé.

Style

The style you follow must convey an impression of confidence, without making you seem a braggart or an egotist. Use of terminology commonly used on the job implies familiarity with the job and the language used. Avoid stating the obvious. Statements like 'This is an application', 'Consider me an applicant for the post', etc. are redundant. Most importantly, ensure that there are no misspelt words, incorrect job titles, typographical errors, and grammatical and punctuation errors. Many companies view such carelessness negatively and upon discovering an error, automatically eliminate an applicant from further consideration.

Mechanics

The physical appearance of the letter communicates something about you. If it conveys a negative impression, it may not be read at all. The size, colour and quality of paper influence the reader's reaction: so do take care of margins, letter format and the arrangement of paragraphs.

Use plain paper for the application letter. While any of the letter formats described in the complete—block style is the most popularly used one. The letter format in Box 9.1 shows the proper format for an application letter.

LETTER PLAN

A letter of application, like most other types of letters, follows a suggested plan. The following elements are included:

- An opening that arouses the reader's interest and makes him want to read the resumé.
- A middle section touching upon your key qualifications and skills.
- A closing section requesting an interview.

Box 9.1: Sample Unsolicited Application Letter

216 Riverview Circle,
Raj Bhavan Road, Hyderabad.
16 June 2001

Mr. William D' Souza, Managing Partner
Samba & Samba Financial Planning Associates
1775 Airport Road
Hyderabad 500 089

Dear Mr. D'Souza:

Congratulations on being featured in this month's Business Standard article about the coming developments in corporate tax planning. After reading about your firm's innovative electronic tax-reporting programmes, I believe my background in computerized accounting and book keeping methods would benefit Samba & Samba.

My degree in accounting and courses in electronic data processing have equipped me to work with computer-based clients like yours. Training in business writing, human relations and psychology should help me achieve a good rapport with them. My advanced studies in tax accounting will enable me to analyse the financial needs from a planning perspective.

Because your company specializes in tax-shelter planning, my work experience could also be beneficial. After 2 years as a part-time book keeper for a securities brokerage firm, I was promoted to full-time financial analyst intern in the corporate investment division. When making recommendations to the firm's corporate clients, I analysed and selected specific tax-shelter programmes. After 3 months, my accomplishments were acknowledged by a substantial salary increase.

Mr. Vikram Saluja, vice president of Citibank, and other references listed on the enclosed resumé will confirm my potential for the staff accountant position.

At a time convenient for you, I would appreciate the opportunity to discuss my qualifications for beginning a career with your company. I will phone you early next Wednesday to see whether we can arrange a meeting at your convenience.

Sincerely,

Satish Kumar

Enclosure

Opening Section

The opening of your application letter will probably 'make or break' the letter, that is, it will decide whether the reader will respond favourably to the request for an interview or not.

There is no one standard opening. The information you want to include varies according to the circumstances. You may name the person from whom you learnt about the job opening, or provide information about how your qualifications fit the job requirements. You may even mention one of the company's significant accomplishments to catch the reader's eye. Whatever type of opening you choose, make sure you include the title of the position for which you are applying in your first paragraph.

In solicited letters of application, it is advisable to mention how you found out about the vacancy. Provide the name of the person who informed you or the publication that listed the vacancy. Being specific will create more interest in the letter, especially if the reader and the person you name in the opening are acquainted. Look at the following three openings:

1. *Please consider me an applicant for the position that I recently learned was available in your company.*
2. *Mr. Ashok Ahyja, an HR Manager, informed me about an opening for an editor in your publishing department.*
3. *Because my diploma in journalism and 3 year's experience on the news desk of a national newspaper qualify me for such a position, please consider me for the post.*

Notice the difference between the first opening and the second and third ones. The first one is weak as it lacks specificity and seems to be written without care. The second and third openings are more effective, as they are more specific, are written from your viewpoint and mention the positions for which the writers are applying.

If you choose an opening that lists your most important qualifications for the job, then again, the you-attitude makes the letter more effective. Look at these examples.

- *I would like to have the opportunity to put my educational and work experience to use as an employee in your company.*
- *Several years of retail work experience in a women's garments boutique, a degree in international marketing and an ability to put in long hours of work would enable me to perform well as the business head of the export division you are seeking.*
- *An ability to communicate well both orally and in writing, a degree in business administration with PGDCA and a six-month live project with a*

software engineering company are the qualifications I have that closely match the requirements of the systems analyst position, open in your company.

The first example is based on the I-attitude, and lacks specificity, which makes it far less effective than the other two openings.

Another way to attract the reader's attention is by opening with a reference to a significant accomplishment of the company. Look at these examples:

- *The article that I recently read about your company has convinced me that your company would be an excellent place for me to begin my career. Please consider me an applicant for any opening in your company.*
- *The recent article about I spat Steel, which appeared in Business Standard, convinces me that the foresight of your managers will allow the company's expansion plans to succeed. Please consider me for the area manager's post advertised in the 23 September issue of The Economic Times.*

Middle Section

This being the section where you discuss your qualifications for the job, it will be the longest one. This section should assure the reader that you are indeed qualified. In developing this section, it is up to you to choose which of the following elements you want to include, after a careful consideration of how appropriate each would be for you and for the job for which you are applying:

- Your understanding of the job requirements.
- Your educational achievements that qualify you for the job.
- Your work experience that helps qualify you for the position.
- Any special qualifications that may give you an edge over other applicants.
- Personal information, such as your marks/grade average, the college activities in which you have participated, honours and awards you have received, evidence of your ability to shoulder responsibility and so on.

As the application letter is ideally limited to one page, focus on your key selling point—something that the reader can use to his advantage.

As mentioned earlier, when reviewing the requirements for the position, don't just state the job requirements—the reader already knows these. Your job is to convince the reader that you have studied the position sufficiently to know that your qualifications match the requirements. Look at this example:

I understand you are looking for a hard-working, ambitious employee.

Does this kind of a statement enhance the effectiveness of your letter? The employer knows he wants a hard-working, ambitious employee. But, how do you lead him to believe that you may be just the person he is looking for? Now, look at this example:

A background in statistics qualifies me as the research coordinator you are seeking, who is required to have an analytical background and to be familiar with statistical applications.

The second example specifies what makes the applicant suitable for the opening, and is therefore more effective.

While summarizing your key qualifications, make sure you present your education and work achievements in such a manner that their significance to the job in question is immediately noticed. As mentioned earlier, do not clutter your letter by enumerating every course you have taken or every job you have held. Focus on the areas that will give you an edge over other the applicants. Do not repeat the facts presented in your resumé, interpret those facts for the reader. Look at the following two statements:

1. *The training I received as a student of business administration will enable me to perform well as an employee in your company.*
2. *The accounting and data processing courses I studied at the Bhartidasan University enabled me to become familiar with accounting theory, procedures and practices, as well as with computerized accounting processes. An understanding of the role of data processing in accounting would enable me to work effectively with clients who have installed computerized accounting systems. Selective courses in written and oral communication will also enable me to communicate effectively with these clients.*

Notice how skillfully the second example connects the applicant's educational qualifications to the job requirements.

While presenting information about your work experience, show how your experience

- will be useful in the job for which you are applying;
- has helped you to develop your skills and made you a responsible, hard-working employee;
- has given you an opportunity to work with others.

If you believe you have special qualities for the position, it may be to your advantage to discuss them. For instance, the ability to speak several languages may be an added qualification when applying for a marketing job in an MNC. But whatever qualities you mention, make sure you do it from a 'you-viewpoint' rather than an 'I-viewpoint'. The employer is looking for that extra something that his organization can use, not for an individual whose biography would make elevating reading.

Be sure to provide all information requested in the job advertisement. If the advertisement asks you to specify the salary you expect, then provide the requested information. Some applicant's who are not comfortable with specifying an amount. Prefer to put something like this 'I would expect a salary commensurate with the requirements of the position and with my qualifications'. If you prefer to specify an amount, make sure you have some idea about what other firms, or may be even the same firm pays for the kind of job you are applying for. Once you know what you can reasonably expect, you can communicate your expectations by saying, '*Given my background, training, the going rates for this position, and the cost of living in Hyderabad, a starting salary of Rs. 18,000 per month would be acceptable*'.

Towards the end of the middle section, refer to the enclosed resumé. Of course, a statement like 'A resumé is enclosed' is unnecessary. A more appropriate reference may be:

'*My work experience, outlined on the enclosed resumé, has taught me valuable lessons about working with others*'.

Closing Section

In the closing section of your letter, your primary task is to ask the reader for a specific action, basically ask for an interview and to make a reply easy. But do not simply ask for an interview that would be too abrupt. To make it sound less so, include other material, such as an offer to provide additional information that the reader may require or the dates on which you might be available for an interview. Take a look at the following examples:

- *May I have an interview on a convenient date?*
- *Additional information about my qualifications for this position can be discussed during an interview, although this letter and the attached resumé do outline several. You can reach me at (040) 8823404 between 9a.m. and 5 p.m. each day of the week to let me know a time that is convenient for you to talk with me about the auditing position.*
- *After you have read my resumé, please call or write to let me know a time that is convenient for you to discuss the chief editor's position with me. Should you need additional information please let me know.*

While the first example sounds rather abrupt, the two other examples motivate the reader to call the applicant for an interview in a tactful manner.

Box 9.1 shows you an effective unsolicited application letter, while Box 9.2 gives you a checklist for application letters which provides, in a nutshell, the important aspects that you must bear in mind when drafting an application letter.

Box 9.2: Checklist for Application Letters.

A. Attention (Opening Paragraph)

1. Open the letter by capturing the reader's attention in a businesslike way:
   a. Summary opening. Present your strongest, most relevant qualifications, with an explanation of how they can benefit the organization.
   b. Name opening. Mention the name of a person who is well known to the reader and who has suggested that you apply for the job.
   c. Source opening. When responding to a job ad, identify the publication i n which the ad appeared and briefly describe how you meet each requirement stated in the ad.
   d. Question opening. Pose an attention—getting question that shows you understand an organization's problem, need or goal and have a genuine desire to help solve or meet it.
   e. News opening. Cite a publicized organizational achievement, contemplated change, or new procedure or product; then link it to your desire to work for the organization.
   f. Personalized opening. Present one of your relevant interests, mention previous experience with the organization, or cite your present position or status as a means of leading into a discussion of why you want to work for the organization.
2. State that you are applying for a job and identify the position or the type of work you seek.

B. Interest and Desire, or Evidence of Qualifications (Next Several Paragraphs)

1. Present your key qualifications for the job, highlighting what is on your resumé: job-related education and training; relevant work experience; and related activities, interests and qualities.
2. Adopt a mature and businesslike tone.
   a. Eliminate boasting and exaggeration.
   b. Back up your claims of ability by citing specific achievements in educational and work settings (or in outside activities).
   c. Demonstrate a knowledge of the organization and a desire to join it by citing its operations or trends in the industry.
3. Link your education, experience and personal qualities to the job requirements.
   a. Relate aspects of your training or work experience to those of the target position.
   b. Outline your educational preparation for the job.
   c. Provide proof that you learn quickly, are a hard worker, can handle responsibility and/or get along well with others.

   d. Present ample evidence of the personal qualities and the work attitudes that are desirable for job performance.
   e. If asked to state salary requirements, provide current salary or a desired salary range, and link it to the benefits of hiring you.
4. Refer the reader to the enclosed resumé.

C. Action (Closing Paragraph)

1. Request an interview at the reader's convenience.
2. Request a screening interview with the nearest regional representative, if company headquarters is some distance away.
3. State your phone number (with area code) and the best time to reach you, to make the interview request easy to comply with, or mention a time when you will be calling to set up an interview.
4. Express appreciation for an opportunity to have an interview.
5. Repeat your strongest qualification, to help reinforce the claim that you have something to offer the organization.

Source: Bovee & Thill, *Business Communication Today* (New York, McGraw Hill, 1995) 372.

10

Writing Effective Memos

In this chapter, we will discuss:

- Fundamentals of Effective Memos
- Types of Memos
- Memos About the Unpleasant
- Persuasive Memos

FUNDAMENTALS OF EFFECTIVE MEMOS

A memo is a written message designed to provide a quick, convenient way for personnel to communicate with each other. Memos can range from informal, handwritten notes to formal, typewritten reports. The former are more common and are often used for handling day-to-day activities like conveying telephone messages, reminding people of upcoming events and responding to inquiries. Formal, typewritten (word processor) memos are used to convey information such as quarterly sales reports, detailed suggestions for cost improvements and analyses of customer concerns.

There are a number of reasons for using memos. First, they are convenient. Second, they usually (not always!) take little time to write or read. Third, they provide a written record for future reference. This explains why millions of organizational memos are written everyday.

OBJECTIVES OF MEMOS

It is not uncommon to find memos so full of errors that they are totally incomprehensible. An ironic state of affairs, considering that memos are supposed to convey information in a direct and efficient manner.

The content of a memo should depend on its objectives. These objectives will help determine the type of memo that should be used: request, confirmation, periodic report, ideas and suggestions, or informal study results. Depending on the audience and writing situation, memos can be either informal or businesslike, short and to the point or detailed; self-promoting or adhering strictly to facts. The overall structure of a memo also varies, depending on the subject and the reader's attitude. Some situations require a deductive approach while other, more delicate, circumstances need an inductive approach.

Organization

Memos are designed to provide information and, often, to get action. Since these messages are usually short and direct (usually, but not always), organization is important. The reader must be able to understand quickly the reason for the message and the action (if any) that is desired (see Box 10.1).

Clarity

Since most memos are designed to be brief and to the point, they are easy to understand. Sometimes, a memo will lack clarity. Examine the vague and unclear memo in Box 10.2.

Note the date on the memo. Will Kiran remember this conversation? It has been many months since their discussion. Now read the improved example in Box 10.3.

Box 10.1: A Well-organized Memo

DATE: 22 November 2000
TO: Subhashini Mehta
FROM: Ravi Kumar
SUBJECT: Strategic Plan Trial Presentation

I have checked on the materials and equipment you will need for your presentation to the board of directors next week. I have learned the following:

1. The agenda will be typed and in your hands by 10 a.m. tomorrow.
2. The transparencies will be completed late Wednesday afternoon. They will be on your desk by 9 a.m. Thursday.
3. The presentation room will have all the audio-visual and support equipment you need.
4. You can use the boardroom on Friday from 9 to 11 a.m. for a trial run of the presentation. There will be five senior managers in attendance. When the presentation is over, they will offer you suggestions and recommendations for the final presentation to the board.
5. If there is anything else you need, I can be reached at extension 242 today and tomorrow.

The second version clarifies Ramesh's topic and sets a time by which the information should be sent. If Kiran does not have the information or cannot get it to Ramesh by Friday, she can tell him.

The lack of clarity in Box 10.2 was due to the vague and general manner in which information was requested. Problems of clarity also arise due to the nature of the language used. Take a look at the memo in Box 10.4.

Yes that's the same memo you read at the beginning of the chapter. Have you deciphered it yet? The memo in Box 10.5 tones down the language and eliminates wordiness and ambiguity.

Box 10.2: A Vague and Unclear Memo

DATE: 1 November 2000
TO: Kiran Kukreja
FROM: Ramesh Singhal
SUBJECT: Our Previous Talk

I would be interested in receiving copies of that material that you and I talked about at the annual meeting last December.

Box 10.3: A Precise, Clear Memo

DATE: 1 November 2000
TO: Kiran Kukreja
FROM: Ramesh Singhal
SUBJECT: Employee Turnover Data

At the annual management meeting last December, you mentioned that you had collected on employee turnover data. Could you send me a copy of this material by Friday? Thanks.

Box 10.4: A Wordy and Ambiguous Memo

DATE: 2 December 2000
TO: Shirin Lakdawalla
FROM: Bairam Pestonjee
SUBJECT: Improving Communication with our Overseas Suppliers

The intercultural concepts that were discussed at the most recent managerial convocation lead me to believe that it would behove you to investigate the causal factors that account for these differences and to determine how we might capitalize on these findings through a detailed analysis of our international management agreements with our overseas suppliers and concessionaires.

Box 10.5: A Direct, Concise and Simple Memo

DATE: 2 December 2000
TO: Shirin Lakdawalla
FROM: Bairam Pestonjee
SUBJECT: Improving Communication with our Overseas Suppliers

As a result of our recent management meeting, I think an evaluation of all contracts with our overseas suppliers and concessionaires is in order. I would like you to find out what can be done to improve our relationships with these people. Please send me your ideas as soon as possible.

Direct, concise and simple—now anyone can understand it. Sadly, many memos circulating in companies require a certified wizard to decipher them. See Exhibit 10.1 for snippets from some 'real' memos.

Sometimes a memo needs to be more than just well written; it requires graphic support. This is often the case when reporting financial or quantitative data. Consider the memo in Box 10.6.

The memo contains the information the reader requested. However, one of two things should be added to the memo. Either the absolute or percentage differences in monthly sales should be computed or a graph of each month's sales should accompany the memo. By themselves the ns are hard to interpret, but a graph would have provided a visual comparison of the results. Graphic support can be an important supplement to a memo containing quantitative information.

TYPES OF MEMOS

Most memos fall into one of five basic categories: request, confirmation, periodic report, ideas and suggestions, and informal study results.

Request Memo

The objective of a request memo is to gain a favourable response to a request. The memo must be written in a convincing way. Consider the following case:

Hirdesh Humayun would like to attend a time management training programme that will be sponsored by the chamber of commerce at a local hotel. The manager has asked Hirdesh to put his request in writing. Box 10.6 depicts Hirdesh's memo.

> **Box 10.6: Poor Example of a Request Memo**
>
> DATE: 5 December 2000
> TO: T M Chopra
> FROM: Hirdesh Humayun
> SUBJECT: Attendance at Time Management Seminar
>
> May I attend the time management seminar that is being offered by the Chamber of commerce next Thursday? Thanks.

The memo is direct and clear, but not suitable from the reader's point of view. As a result, it may even fail to achieve its objective. Consider the manager's situation. If many of the departmental personnel make a similar request, the manager may have to limit the number who can attend. To achieve its objective, Hirdesh's memo will have to be like a sales message. The memo should motivate the reader to take the desired action. The guidelines given below should be followed:

- The request should be stated clearly.
- The reasons for the request should be presented.
- If any financial costs are involved, they should be explained.
- All expenses should be justified.
- Recommendations for action should be presented.
- Throughout the memo tact and diplomacy should be used.

If the memo is persuasively written, it should be easy for the reader to say 'yes'.

Following these six guidelines, Hirdesh's memo has been improved—see Box 10.7.

Notice the difference between the first and second drafts of the memo. The second version reminds the reader of a previous conversation during which the seminar was discussed. This serves as an introduction to the main memo.

The reasons are then presented persuasively—showing indirect and direct benefits to the company (i.e. reader-oriented). Finally, there is a request for action.

Periodic Report Memo

Periodic report memos—monthly cost control reports, quarterly sales reports—are submitted at regular intervals.

Box 10.7: Good Example of a Request Memo.

DATE: 5 December 2000
TO: T M Chopra
FROM: Hirdesh Humayun
SUBJECT: Attendance at Time Management Seminar

As I mentioned to you last week, the Chamber of Commerce is sponsoring a time management seminar. It is being conducted by one of the professors in the management department of unpaid university. The seminar will be held at the chamber and because of the low overhead involved, the participant fee is only Rs 500 for the entire day.

Since the personnel cutback 6 months ago, I have been working without an assistant. A time management seminar would help me improve my productivity and reduce some of the work backlog. The attached brochure presents the contents of the seminar. Many of these topics are productivity oriented.

Five hundred rupees is an excellent price for the training. I have checked with the personnel and learned that the average time management seminar conducted by national training groups cost between Rs 2000 and Rs 2500 per day. In addition, these seminars are at distant locations requiring travel and hotel expenses.

Considering the value of this training and the low cost to the firm, I would like approval to attend the seminar. Although registration closes on Wednesday, 13 December, I am sure that the enrollment cap of 30 will be filled before the end of this week. May I hear from you before Friday.

Since these memos are written frequently, they are designed and preprinted so that the writer can complete them quickly. There are three helpful guidelines for constructing a periodic report memo:

1. The memo should be designed as a fill-in form on which data can be entered quickly.
2. The form should be designed so that it can be duplicated and reused.
3. If narrative or descriptive commentary is necessary, a place should be provided on the form.

The value of a periodic memo is best illustrated with a comparison. Take a look at the memo in Box 10.8 and then see how the readability and comprehension is improved by the style used in Box 10.9.

The memo in Box 10.8 is difficult to read, grasp and make comparisons. But the report memo in Box 10.9 is concise, comprehensive and easy to understand. And every quarter all that the manager has to do is enter the relevant data.

Box 10.8: Periodic Report Memo: Poor Formatting Results in a Hard-to-Read Memo

DATE: 6 April 2000
TO: Azim Azad
FROM: Pankaj Pinto
SUBJECT: Quarterly Sales Report for the Southern Region for January1–March 31

During the first quarter in the Kerala-Karnataka area, T. Ramesh made sales of Rs 184,612. This was an increase of Rs 22,435 over the first quarter of last year. C. Parekh had sales of Rs 122,655. This was his first quarter with us. B. Bharat had sales of Rs 144,446. This was Rs 35,442 less than this quarter last year. A Elijah had sales of Rs 202,978. This was an increase of Rs 47,990 over last year.

In the Tamil Nadu area, W. Pavan had sales of Rs 124,326. T. Chopra had sales of Rs 63,488. W. Singh had sales of Rs 101,496. Each of these people has been with us for less than 6 months.

In the Maharashtra–A.P.–Orissa area, J. Krishnamurti had sales of Rs 224,116, which was an increase of Rs 51,406. R. Kumar had sales of Rs 175,283, which represents a decline of Rs 31,509. D. Lapang had sales of Rs 258,407, which was an increase of Rs 68,407. B. Somaiah had sales of Rs 231,663, which was an increase of Rs 19,332. T. Saiwai had sales of Rs 109,582, which was a dramatic decline of Rs 81,764. However, it should be pointed out that he was sick for 4 weeks during this quarter.

Ideas and Suggestions Memo

Sometimes memos are used to convey ideas or suggestions. Very often managers ask subordinates for suggestions for tackling certain problems. In such instances, an ideas and suggestions memo is required. Follow the guidelines listed below for writing this type of memo:

Write directly—the manager would not have asked for ideas unless he thought that the writer had something to offer.

- Begin with positive comments about the current situation (no one likes to be shot down), and then tactfully present suggestions for change.
- Group ideas according to subject and use headings to highlight them.
- Be specific and do not stray off the point.

Read the memo in Box 10.10 and identify its drawbacks. What is wrong with this memo?

Box 10.10: Four Examples of an Ideas and Suggestions Memo

DATE: 15 May 2000
TO: Krishna Parthasarthy
FROM: Seema Pal
SUBJECT: Suggestions for Reducing Absenteeism and Turnover.

Thank you for asking for suggestions regarding how we can reduce absenteeism and turnover. I think some of the areas we should examine include competitive salaries, the benefit package, job redesign and union relations. I am sure that there are many other areas that warrant attention, and you know them a lot better than I do. I simply throw these out as some that should be considered. I'll be more than happy to go along with whatever you decide to do.

Box 10.11: Good Example of an Ideas and Suggestions Memo

DATE: 15 May 2000
TO: Krishna Parthasarthy
FROM: Seema Pal
SUBJECT: Suggestions for Reducing Absenteeism and Turnover

I am happy to respond to your request about suggestions for reducing absenteeism and turnover. The current rate of absenteeism and tardiness is not much higher than the industry average, so we do not need to make radical changes. However, I believe we should take the following steps.

COMPETITIVE SALARIES

In most jobs, we praise competitive salaries. However, we are below the industry average in our wage rates for incoming secretarial help and for unit managers with 3 to 5 years experience. Since these are the two groups in which we are having the greatest turnover, we must raise their salaries to those of the competitor.

BENEFIT PACKAGE

Our health benefit package is too limited. Coverage of major medical problems such as hospital confinement is excellent. However, the package provides only minimal assistance for routine expenses such as prescription medicines or doctor's visits. Over 40 per cent of the people leaving our firm say that the medical insurance package is poor. We need a package that is at least as good as those of our major competitor.

JOB REDESIGN

More attention needs to be given to redesigning jobs. In particular, the following three things should be done:

1. Start giving the works whether autonomy over their work.
2. Increase the amount of the feedback in the jobs so that the personnel can tell for themselves when their work is satisfactory.
3. Investigate the value of installing quality circles throughout the organization, especially on the shop floor.

UNION INTERFACE

Greater attention needs to be focused on union relations. If we can win union support for the new medical insurance benefit package and job

Box 10.12: Poor Example of a Memorandum about Poor Job Performance

12 June 2000
Amar Patnaik
[1]SUBSTANDARD PERFORMANCE
[2]Your presentation to josh company representatives this morning was below our standards. [3]The following weaknesses were apparent:

- Too technical
- Participants had no chance for hands-on experience.
- Failure to get participants to respond to questions for fear that they would look foolish.

[4]I insist that the presentation be revised before the same firm sends another group of representatives to visit us next week. [5]You might check to see whether our training consultant can be helpful.

Anjali Joshi

Marketing Manager

1. As a subject line, these words immediately put the reader on the defensive.
2. Emphasizes a negative thought by placing it in the first sentence and using negative language.
3. Emphasizes negatives with negative words (weakness and failure). Emphasizes unpleasant points by using tabulation and enumeration.
4. Seems unnecessarily demanding ('I insist').
5. Unnecessarily weak in referring to action ('You might check').

redesign changes, we should be able to reduce absenteeism and turnover there are two things we can do to gain this support:

1. Meet with the union representative and discuss what we want to do.
2. Form a committee with the union representatives to institute these changes.

If you would like to discuss any of these ideas, please give me a call.

- The writer is too general. She has not pointed out what the company should do to tackle its problems.
- She is more concerned with keeping her boss happy than with presenting useful suggestions.

Box 10.13: Good Example of a Memorandum about Poor Job Performance

12 June 2000
Amar Patnaik

[1] NEXT WEEK'S SALES PRESENTATION TO JOSH COMPANY

[2] Your Presentation to Josh Company representatives this morning was thorough and clear to me

[3] Because you were so well informed and organized, participants who were already somewhat familiar with our system were able to benefit greatly. [4] Most of them, though, would have gained more from a less technical discussion that involved hands-on experience and encouraged spontaneous questions.

[5] Before next week's presentation, ask our training consultant (Padma Kapoor) for suggestions. [6] She has excellent ideas and access to the latest in audio-visual equipment.

Anjali Joshi

Marketing manager

---

1. As a subject line, these words assist in achieving a positive tone. A discussion of qualities desired in next week's presentation can have a much more positive tone than a discussion about the weaknesses of this morning's presentation.

2. Uses positive language to introduce the topic.

3. Lets compliment precede criticism. By recognizing positive qualities, the supervisor establishes objectivity and reduces the sting of comments about negatives.

4. Identifies ways in which improvement can be made.

5 and 6. Close with a helpful recommendation.

Now read the memo in Box 10.12 and see how powerful it is.

Much better, isn't it? The opening paragraphs define the problem tactfully. The recommendations are grouped by headings, and each is carefully explained. The conclusion is action oriented. The writer indicates how the recommendations can be implemented.

PERSUASIVE MEMOS

It is fairly simple to write an 'ideas and suggestions' memo when the audience is receptive to our ideas. But it is quite another story when attempting to convince an uninterested or even potentially antagonistic audience. Such a situation poses a communication challenge. Box 10.14 describes one such situation.

Consider the context of the memo in Box 10.15. A few months back the president of the company had indicated his opposition to any changes in

Box 10.14: Dealing With a Sensitive Audience

Let us say you are preparing a memo to your supervisor, you are hoping for his approval of a cost-saving project you want to spearhead. Something fairly similar to it had been tried years ago; it failed miserably, embarrassing your supervisor and his supervisor. You know that seeking approval is an uphill task, but you believe in yourself and the project. What tone should this sensitive memo take?

The temptation may be to position your project point-for-point in contrast to the old one, pounding on the relative merits of yours in an effort to convey its superiority.

Resist this temptation as you would a term paper over the mid-term holidays. Never directly mention the other project in your memo; memories of its failure may be keen, and direct comparisons will be counter productive to the objectivity you want to elicit in your readers. Rather, emphasize the strength of your plan by stressing features of it which are designed to avoid known pitfalls.

Your supervisor and his supervisor will get the message, and you will get your project. The moral to take away from all of this: do not stand on the grave of a bad idea to sell a new one.

James F. Hurley

Senior Vice President

CalFed Inc.

Box 10.15: Good Example of a Persuasive Memorandum

DATE: H B Suman, President
TO: Raj Ganesh, Production Manager
FROM: 1 March 2000
SUBJECT: Proposal to Reduce Parking Congestion at Peak Hours

Although employee morale is already high, we can do something to make it still higher.

Almost 1,000 of our employees come to work and leave at the same time. With more than 600 cars in our parking lot, about 30 minutes are required to clear it each evening. Having worked hard for 8 hours without wasting any company time, employees experience a challenge to their morale when a half-hour of their time is wasted.

Many employees, especially production workers, begin their day with a negative pull on their morale: They must arrive at the parking lot a half-hour early so they can begin work on schedule.

The following schedule changes would go a long way towards solving the problem (without cost to Kapoor Industries).

work schedules. But the production manager feels that parking congestion at peak hours can be reduced only by altering work schedules. To achieve his objective, the production manager constructs a persuasive, inductive memo to win over the audience.

Note that the subject line does not reveal how reduction in congestion is to be achieved. If the president reads 'change in work schedules' in the subject line, the memo is off to a bad start. Knowing the president's concern about morale, and recognizing the problem's impact on his morale, the production manager uses morale as an appeal. In fact, the word morale is repeated often throughout the memo.

For effective communication, business people must write clear, logically developed memos. In general, memos that contain good news or neutral information should be written deductively, whereas memos that contain bad news or are intended to persuade should be written inductively.

Production and Plant Staff

Change work hours of production and plant staff. Instead of beginning at 8 a.m. and leaving at 4:30 p.m., begin at 7:30 a.m. and leave at 4:00 p.m. This change would affect about 700 employees. It has support from the employee council.

Office and Management Staffs

Make no change in work hours for office and management staffs. By the time they arrive at the parking lot, production and plant workers would be already settled in their parking spaces. By the time they leave, traffic lanes should be clear for fast departure.

By making these changes, Kapoor Industries would again demonstrate its concern for employee's problems. They would be appreciative, and we should detect a positive influence on their morale.

After you have considered this change, I would be pleased to survey production and plant personnel about their willingness to begin and leave work half an hour early.

And before putting pen to paper, bear in mind the words of a senior executive: '*Ask yourself if the information in the memo you are about to write can be communicated just as effectively with a phone call or a brief meeting. Too many memos is a signal to others that you are overreaching and under-achieving*'.

11

Structure and Layout of Letters

In this chapter, we will discuss:

- Punctuation Styles and Letter Formats
- Formats
- Standard Letter Parts
- Special Letter Parts
- Memorandum Formats

Imagine you are an HR manager in a medium-sized firm, which recently put out an advertisement for sales representatives. The company needs three people. You get nearly 500 application letters. As you begin sifting through them, you get one that is written on dirty, yellowing paper. Another one has such a cluttered look that you know reading it will take quite some effort. How would you react to such letters? In all probability, you would put them aside, and go back to them, only if you did not find enough interesting letters from the ones that have a better appearance. After all, it is the appearance that makes the first impression. So it is well worth taking that extra effort to see that your letter—any letter—has an attractive appearance. Let us look at some of the factors that help you to do that.

Paper: Use good quality; bond paper that does not yellow very fast. Business letters are most often written on white papers, but some businesses use pastel or grey stationery.

Personalization: Business letter are often personalized through the use of letterhead stationery. The letterhead contains the company's name, address, telephone number, fax number, e-mail address and the name of the department that is sending the correspondence. The letterhead is usually centred at the top of the page, but it may also be placed to the left or right. In some cases, the letter head appears at the bottom of the page. Letterheads should be distinctive without being too outlandish.

Appearance: To ensure the letter has a neat appearance, use proper spacing and punctuation. People's initials should have a period after each letter, but organizational abbreviations such as IBM should not. Letters should be balanced on the page with approximately equal margins. A letter which is very short should have wider side margins than long letters.

FORMATS

The three letter formats that are usually used are the block, the modified block and the simplified block.

Box 11.1: Block Format with Open Punctuation

The Society of Bird Watchers
Juhu Chapter, Bird Watchers' Lane, Juhu

DATE LINE 24 February 2001
INSIDE ADDRESS Mr. Ajith M. Suri
1938 Andher Nagari Avenue
Andheri, Bombay 6543219
SALUTATION Dear Mr. Suri,

Your recent article, 'Are Bird Watchers Becoming an Endangered Species?' has attracted the attention of all bird lovers in the city.

BODY As you must be aware, there are at least 13 bird lovers' associations in various parts of this city. Many members of these different associations now feel that there should be greater coordination among these bodies. As a step in this direction, we have made arrangements for an informal get-together. About 200 members will attend this dinner meeting. They would be glad to meet you and interested in hearing you discuss 'Threats to Bird Watching in a Metropolis'.

By accepting this invitation, you will be able to meet other bird lovers in the city. We are sure you will find many who share your concerns about the problems faced by bird watchers in this city. The meeting will be at Hum Panchchi Ek Dal Ke Hotel on 6 March at 5 p.m. We promise you a pleasant evening and an attentive audience.

We would appreciate having, with your acceptance, a photograph to be printed in the programme.

COMPLIMENTARY CLOSE Sincerely
SIGNATURE BLOCK Lalita Popat
REFERENCE INITIALS tw
Assistant Manager

Block

In this format all lines begin at the left margin. Box 11.1 shows a letter in block format with open punctuation.

Modified Block

The modified block is the traditional letter format and is still used in many companies. The date line, complimentary close, and signature block begin at, or near the horizontal centre of the page. All other lines begin at the left margin. Look at the letter in modified block format and mixed punctuation shown in Box 11.2.

Box 11.2: Modified Block Format with Mixed Punctuation

DATTE'S Malkauns Road
Small Engines New Bombay 7702678

DATE LINE 4 February 2001
INSIDE ADDRESS Mr. Asim Banerjee
Calcutta, 6282288
Andheri, Bombay 6543219
SALUTATION Dear Mr. Banerjee:

Vinayak motors are among the most dependable small electric motors manufactured in India today. Here at Datte's Small Engines, we believe that the right size Vinayak engine for the particular job is critical.

BODY The three-month warranty with the Vinayak motors applies only if the motor is used under normal operating conditions. Your pipe size (3/15 inch), the large distance between your pool and the filtering system (100 feet), and the size of your pool (50 by 60 feet) placed undue stress on the 2.5 horse-power motor. Your sales receipt indicates that a 3.5 horse power motor was recommended based on our evaluation of your needs.

Our sales forces will be happy to show you the 3.5 horse-power Vinayak motor. This powerful motor should provide clear, sparkling water for the enjoyment of your family.

COMPLIMENTARY CLOSE Sincerely
SIGNATURE BLOCK Abdul Karim
REFERENCE INITIAL ms Manager

Simplified Block

This is an efficient letter format. Like the block format, all lines begin at the left margin, but the salutation and complimentary close are omitted and a subject line is required. The subject line is placed a double space below the inside address and a double space above the body. Box 11.3 shows a letter in simplified block format.

Box 11.3: Simplified Block Format

Moon Side Cable Television
Telephone 824586

DATE LINE 15 February 2001
INSIDE ADDRESS Mr. Raja Achanta
267 Ajanata Apartments
Riverside Avenue-Bandra.
SUBJECT LINE Change in cable service
SALUTATION Dear Mr. Banerjee:

Some important changes in your cable television service will begin 1 March 2001. We will rearrange our channel line-up and introduce a change in rate. These changes are necessary to maintain programming selection.

BODY
Our new monthly rates are as follows:

Basic Service	Rs 150
Extended Service	Rs 180
Premium Service	Rs 250

With these changes, the cost of our extended package (all channels except premium for pay) is still only Rs 6 per day, less than the cost of a cup of coffee and a samosa.

Our employees are committed to providing you with the best quality and variety of cable television, including education, sports, religion and public affairs programming. Please call us if we can be of additional service to you.

SIGNATURE BLOCK Ashok Gehlot
REFERENCE INITIAL OMITTED Systems Manager

STANDARD LETTER PARTS

- Heading and Date
- Inside Address
- Salutation
- Body
- Complimentary Close
- Signature Block
- Reference Initials

Heading and Date

The heading contains the writer's address. Many businesses incorporate the information in the letterhead. The date is typed in two to six lines below the last line the letterhead and can be placed at the left-hand margin, in the centre or ending at the right-hand margin. The month should be spelled out, not abbreviated, followed by the day and year. It is better to avoid putting the date in numerals: 12.9.2000 international correspondence, this creates confusion about whether the month mentioned first or the day.

If the letter is written on blank paper, the writer's address must come immediate above the date. The writer's name is omitted because it appears in bold in the signature.

Inside Address

The inside address usually begins four spaces below the dateline. It includes a person or professional title, the name of the person and the company to whom the letter is being sent, and the complete address. Box 11.4 shows you how the heading and inside address are arranged on a page with a letterhead and on a blank page.

Salutation

The salutation is a greeting that precedes the body of the letter. It is placed in double space below the inside address. There are a number of acceptable salutations. If the letter is being sent to a specific person, the individual's name should be used: *Dear Mr. Kulshreshtha*. If the writer is on a first-name basis with the recipient, and it is appropriate to use it, an informal salutation is acceptable: Dear Rina. It is a little more difficult to decide how to word a salutation in a letter addressed to a group, to an unknown person, or to an unnamed person in a particular position. For example, if you do not know

Box 11.4: A Letter Heading and a Plain Paper Heading

Letterhead Heading	Heading on Plain Paper
Graphic Design Advertising East Hill, Kolkata 12 August 2001	East Hill, Calcutta 12 August 2001
Ms. Dhanno Jaiswal Jaiswal & Associates 2988 Rayees Marg Ahmedabad 784657	Ms. Dhanno Jaiswal Jaiswal & Associates 2988 Rayees Marg Ahmedabad 784 657
Dear Ms. Dhanno:	Dear Ms. Dhanno:

whether the recipient is a male or a female, use the whole name or omit the salutation to avoid offending the person. Sometimes, the recipient's official title is used: *Dear Accounts Officer*. In the case of sales letters or announcements that are sent out to many people, a general salutation may be used: *Dear Customer; Dear Policyholder*.

Some writers now use a salutopening on the salutation line. This is an opening line that omits 'Dear', begins with the first few words from the body of the message, and incorporates the reader's name. After this, there is a double space and the body of the letter continues. Here is an example:

Thank you, Mr. Brown, (Salutopening)
For your prompt payment of your bill (Body)

Body

The body of the letter contains the message. It begins a double space below the salutation. The text is usually single spaced, with double spacing between the paragraphs. It is best to keep the first and last paragraphs to 5 lines or less so that reader interest is maintained. Other paragraphs can have 8 to 10 lines each. Tables, numbered items, long quotations and other such material should be set up in such way that they are easy to read. Two ways of doing this are underlining key words phrases and leaving extra space around such material to set it off. For example,

(A)	Mr. Aditya Bajaj, President Birlaj Communications	Mr. Aditya Bajaj, President Birlaj Communications

(B) Amar Kashyap, Manager
Quality Control Division
Title on the Same Line

Amar Kashyap, Manager,
Manager, Quality Control Division.
Title on the Next Line

Complimentary Close

This is a phrase that closes the letter—much like saying goodbye at the end of conversation. When you choose a complimentary close, make sure that it reflects the formality of your relationship with the reader. The most commonly used closure '*Sincerely*' is considered neutral, and is thus suited to most business correspondent '*Yours truly*', '*Cordially*' '*Cordially yours*', and '*Sincerely Yours*' are the most commonly used closes. Capitalize only the first word of the complimentary close a position it a double space below the body. The complimentary close and the salutation as mentioned earlier are omitted in the simplified block style.

Signature Block

The writer's name usually comes four spaces below the complimentary close as in the simplified block letter). The writer's signature goes into the space provided the writer is speaking legally for the company, the firm's name is typed in capital letters three spaces below the complimentary close and the writer's name is typed four spaces below that, with the person's title on the next line. Sometimes the title is put in the same line as the name.

Reference Initials

The initials of the person who has keyed in or typed the letter appears in lowercase double space below the signature block. Reference initials are omitted when the letter is keyed in by the writer himself. However, certain companies insist that the initials of all people involved in writing a letter be included in the reference initials line so the writers can be identified in case of litigation.

SPECIAL LETTER PARTS

So far, we have looked at the standard features of business letters. However, these may have several other parts like (i) mailing notation, (ii) attention line, (iii) reference line, (iv) subject line, (v) second-page heading, (vi) enclosure notation, (vii) number of copies and (viii) postscript

Mailing Notation

A mailing notation is used to indicate either how the letter was sent, that is, certified—or how the letter is to be handled—confidential, personal, etc.

The notation be typed in capital letters or underlined and can be placed at the top or bottom of the letter. If it is put at the top, it should be either above the inside address on the left-hand side or just below the date on the right-hand side (in the modified block format). If placed at the bottom, it should be either below the copy notation or below whatever is the last notation.

Attention Line

The attention line directs a letter to a particular person—' Attention Ms Kamalakshi'—or a position in the company—'Attention Personnel Manager'—or a department—'Attention Personnel Department'. Box 11.5 shows you the position of the attention line.

Reference Line

A reference line—'Re: contract 248-2983'—directs the reader to previous files or documents. It is usually put a double space below the inside address.

Subject Line

The subject line tells the reader what the letter is about. It is generally used in the simplified block letter. In other formats, it is optional. The subject

Box 11.5: Special Letter Parts Page 1

Spencer & Taylor Ltd.
37 Chowrangee Lane , Kolkata
(033) 5567824

MAILING NOTATION	19 January 2001 FACSIMILE
ATTENTION LINE	Attention Ms. Janaki Menon Communication Systems, Inc. Modal Building, Room 250 Hyderabad AP 500 082
REFERENCE LINE	RE: Engagement No.39-29-3773 Ladies and Gentlemen:
SUBJECT LINE	ENGAGEMENT AGREEMENT

Spencer Taylor is pleased to confirm our arrangements to audit the financial statements of Communication Systems, Inc. for the year ended 30 June 2001

line is keyed in a double space below the salutation. If the modified block style is used then the subject line may be centred. In the example shown in Box 11.6 the word 'subject' is omitted. This is often done because its position above the body clearly identifies its function.

Second-page Heading

The second and successive pages of multi-page letters and memoranda are keyed in on plain paper. A heading on the second and successive pages identifies them as a continuation of the first page. The heading includes the name of the person or company to whom the message is sent, the page number and the date.

The heading is usually put six lines from the top edge of the paper. The body of the letter starts a double space after the heading.

Box 11.6: Special Letter Parts Page 2

SECOND-PAGE HEADING	Communications systems, Inc. Page 2 19 January 2001

Anita Shrivastav has been assigned as the audit manager in charge of your audit examination. Please review the enclosed preliminary time schedule she has developed and direct your questions to her at 5567824, extension 25.

We at Spencer & Taylor look forward to providing these and other quality professional services to you.

	Sincerely,
	Azhagappa Veerappan
	Audit Partner,
REFERENCE INITIALS	cf
ENCLOSURE NOTATION	Enclosure: Audit Agreement
COPY NOTATION	C Mr. Atul Dadiwala
POSTSCRIPT	Our annual tax update has been scheduled for March 5–6, 2- . You will receive an agenda from the tax department, just as soon as all details have been finalized.

ENCLOSURE NOTATION

An enclosure nation is used when papers or documents like brochures, price lists or résumés accompany the letter. This notation is keyed in a double space below the reference initials. Use the plural form (Enclosures) if more than one document is enclosed. Box 11.6 shows an enclosure notation that specifies the item enclosed.

Copy Notation

A copy notation is used when people other than the addressee are sent copies of the correspondence. The notation is placed two lines below the reference initials or enclosure notation. The different copy notations are: c (copy), xc (xerox copy), cc (carbon copy) or pc (photocopy). The copy notation is omitted when a copy of a letter is sent to someone without the recipient's knowledge. A bcc (blind copy notation) is keyed in on all file copies.

Postscript

The last item that appears on the letter, the postscript, was earlier used to include information that was omitted from the letter. However, with word processing software making retriev ing and editing letters a simple task, the postscript no longer serves this purpose. Today postscripts are largely used to emphasize something. For instance, a sales letter may use a postscript to underline the central selling point. The postscript is keyed in a double space below the last notation or the signature block if no notations are used. Some writers feel that as its position clearly identifies its functions, you need not begin with PS. But others prefer to use the notation PS: before the postscript.

12

The Framework of a Report

In this chapter, we will discuss:

- The Elements of a Report
- The Text of a Report

When businesspeople speak of reports, they are, in general, thinking of written, factual accounts that objectively communicate information about some aspect of the business. In a sense, reports constitute a managerial tool. Even the most capable managers must rely on other people to observe events or collect information and 'report' to them. Managers are often too far away to oversee everything themselves, or they don't have the time. In addition, they lack the specialized background required to research and evaluate certain subjects.

The goal when developing a report for such an audience is to make the information as clear and convenient as possible. To achieve clarity and readability, the elements or components of the report must be carefully crafted and demarcated and the body (or text) of the report must be developed in a logical and focused manner.

THE ELEMENTS OF A REPORT

The 'elements' of a report refer to those components that are usually included in a formal business report. Most organizations have their own format preferences. You should therefore study the style guide used in your organization. If there is no style guide, study a few of the reports in your organization's files. Successful reports are the best guides. As always, when you make decisions about your written documents, your reader's needs are your main concern. Table 12.1 illustrates the six most common uses of reports.

Table 12.1 The Six Most Common Uses of Reports

Purpose of Report	Common Examples	Preparation and Distribution	Features
To monitor control operations	Plans, operating reports and personal activity reports	Internal reports move upward on a recurring basis; external reports go to selected audiences	**Format:** Standard memo or preprinted form **Style:** Telegraphic **Organization:** Topical **Order:** Direct
To implement policies and procedures	Lasting guidelines, position papers	Internal reports move downward on a nonrecurring basis	**Format:** Matches policies and procedures manual **Style:** Fully developed text **Organization:** Topical **Order:** Direct
To comply with regulatory requirements	Reports for the Income Tax Department, government, Environmental Agencies and other industry regulators	External reports are sent on a recurring basis	**Format:** Standardized, perhaps preprinted form **Style:** Skeletal **Organization:** To follow reader's instructions **Order:** Direct
To obtain new business or funding	Sales proposals	External reports are sent on a nonrecurring basis	**Format:** Letter or manuscript **Style:** Fully developed solution **Organization:** Problem solution **Order:** Commonly direct
To document client works	Interim progress reports and final reports	External reports are sent on a nonrecurring basis	**Format:** Letter or manuscript **Style:** Fully developed text **Organization :** Around sequential steps or key findings **Order:** Usually direct
To guide decisions	Research reports, justification reports and troubleshooting reports	Internal reports move upward on a nonrecurring basis	**Format:** Memo or manuscript **Style:** Fully developed text **Organization:** Around conclusions or logical arguments **Order:** Direct or indirect

The Letter of Transmittal

The letter of transmittal introduces the purpose and contents of the report to the principal reader, usually (but not always) the person who requested the report. The letter is attached to the report or simply placed on top of it. Some organizations prefer a memo format if the report is intra-organizational.

The letter of transmittal (or memo) gives you an opportunity to emphasize whatever you feel your reader will find particularly important or interesting in the attached materials. It also enables you to point out any errors or omissions in the materials. For example, you might want to include some information that was gathered after the report was typed or printed.

Transmittal letters generally contain most of the following elements:

- A statement of the title, and if necessary, the purpose of the report.
- A statement of who authorized or commissioned the project, and when.
- A statement of the methods used in the project (if they are noteworthy) or of the principal results, conclusions and recommendations.
- An acknowledgment of any assistance you received in preparing the material.
- A gracious offer to assist in interpreting the material or in carrying out further projects.

The transmittal letter/memo is informal and conversational (uses personal pronouns) in style.

The Title Page

The only difficulty in creating the title page is to think of a good title. The other blocks of information—the date of submission, the names and positions of the writer (or organization) and the principal reader (or organization)—are simply identifying information.

A good title is sufficiently informative without being unwieldy. It answers two basic questions: what is the subject of the report? and what type of report is it? Take a look at the following effective titles:

These descriptive titles identify the subject, and by stating the recommendation they indicate that it is a 'recommendation' report. A convenient way to define the type of report is to use a generic term such as *analysis, recommendation, summary, review, guide or instructions*. For example,

Open Sea Pollution-Control Devices: A summary
An Analysis of the Tata 1013 Packager

Wherever possible, however, use a descriptive title.

In some organizations, a title page is preceded by a title fly. The title fly is a plain sheet of paper with only the title on it. It is not really necessary, but it adds a touch of formality to the report.

The Abstract

An abstract is a brief technical summary—usually no more than 200 words—of the report. The abstract of a report is directed primarily to readers who are familiar with the technical subject and need to know whether to read the full report. So, when writing an abstract you can use technical terminology freely and refer to advanced concepts in your field.

Because abstracts can be useful before and after a report is read—and can even be read in place of the report—they are duplicated and kept on file in many divisions of the organization. And of course a copy of the abstract is attached to or placed within the report.

The two basic types of abstracts are generally called descriptive and informative abstracts. The *descriptive abstract*, sometimes called the topical or table of contents abstract, does only what its name implies. It simply describes the topics covered in the table of contents, giving equal coverage to each. So in this type of abstract the research methods, for example, would be mentioned even if they were not the focus of the report.

The *informative abstract* presents the major information that the report conveys. Instead of merely conveying all the topics in a superficial manner, it states the problem, the scope and methods (if appropriate), and the major results, conclusions or recommendations.

The basic structure of the informative abstract includes the following three elements:

1. The identifying information. The name of the report, the writer and perhaps the writer's department.
2. The problem statement. One or two sentences that define the problem or need that led to the project. Without an adequate problem statement to guide them, many readers will be unable to understand the abstract.
3. The important findings. The final three or four sentences—the biggest portion of the abstract—state the crucial information the report contains. Generally, this means some combination of results, conclusions, recommendations and implications for other projects. Sometimes, however, the abstract presents other information. For instance, many technical projects focus on new or unusual methods for achieving results that have already been obtained through other means. In such a case, the abstract will focus on the methods, not the results.

The Table of Contents

This element is crucial to the report because it enables different readers to turn to specific pages to find the information they want. No matter how well organized the report itself may be, a table of contents that does not make the structure clear will be ineffective.

Because a report usually has no index, the table of contents will provide the only guide to the report's structure, coverage and pagination. The headings listed in the table of contents are identical to the headings that appear in the report itself. To create an effective table of contents, therefore, you must first make sure the report has effective headings—and that it has enough of them. If the table of contents shows no entry for five or six pages, the report could probably be divided into additional subunits. In fact, some tables of contents have a listing of every page in the report.

The List of Illustrations

A list of illustrations is a table of contents for the figures and tables of a report. If the report contains figures, but not tables, the list is called a *list of figures*. If the report contains tables but not figures, the list is called a *list of tables*. If the report contains both figures and tables, figures are listed separately, before the list of tables, and the two lists together are called *a list of illustrations*.

The Executive Summary

The executive summary (sometimes called the epitome, the *executive overview*, the *management summary* or the *management overview*) is a one-page condensation of the report. Its audience is made up of managers who rely on executive summaries to cope with the tremendous amount of paper crossing their desk every day. Managers do not need or want a deep or detailed understanding of the various projects undertaken in their organizations; what managers do need is a broad understanding of the projects and how they fit into a coherent whole. Consequently a one-page (double spaced) maximum for the executive summary has become almost an unwritten standard.

The special needs of managers dictate a two-part structure for the executive summary:

1. **Background.** Because managers are not technically competent in the writer's field, the background of the project is discussed clearly and completely. The specific problem is stated explicitly.
2. **Major findings and implications.** Managers are not interested in the details of the project, so the methods—often the largest portion of the report—rarely receive more than one or two sentences. The conclusions and recommendations, however, are discussed in a full paragraph.

For instance, if the research and development division at an automobile manufacturer has created a composite material that can replace steel in car axles, the technical details of the report might deal with the following kinds of questions:

- How was the composite devised?
- What are its chemical and mechanical structures?
- What are its properties?

The managerial implications, on the other hand, involve other kinds of questions:

- Why is this composite better than steel?
- How much do the raw materials cost? Are they readily available?
- How difficult is it to make the composite? Are there physical limitations to the amount we can make?

.....The executives do not care about chemistry; they only want to know how this project can help them make a better product for less money. And since they are no specialists, writers must avoid or downplay specialized vocabulary and explain the subject without referring to advanced concepts.

The placement of the executive summary highlights its importance. The current practice in business and industry is to place the executive summary before the detailed discussion. To highlight the importance of the executive summary further, it is listed in the table of contents in the same format as the major headings.

The Glossary and List of Symbols

A glossary is an alphabetical list of definitions. Such a list is particularly useful if you are addressing a multiple audience that includes readers who will not be familiar with the technical vocabulary used in your report.

Instead of slowing down the detailed discussion by defining technical terms as they appear, you can use an asterisk or some other form of notation to inform your readers that the term is defined in the glossary. A footnote at the bottom of the page on which the first asterisk appears serves to clarify the system for the readers.

Although the glossary is generally placed near the end of the report, right before the appendixes, it can also be placed right after the table of contents. This placement is appropriate if the glossary is brief (less than a page) and defines terms that are essential for managers who are likely to read the body of the report (see Box 12.1).

Box 12.1: A Sample of Glossary

GLOSSARY

Byte: a binary character operated upon as a unit and generally, shorter than a computer word.

error message: an indication that an error has been detected by the system

Hard copy: in computer graphics, a permanent copy of a display image that can be separated from a display device. For example, a display image recorded on paper.

Parameter: a variable that is given a constant value for a specified application and that may denote that application.

Record length: the number of words or characters forming a record.

Box 12.2: A Sample List of Symbols

CRT	cathode-ray tube
Hz	hertz
rcvr	receiver
SNR	signal-to-noise ratio
uhf	ultrahigh frequency
vhf	very high frequency

A list of symbols is structured like a glossary, but instead of defining words and phrases, it defines the symbols used in the report (so that readers do not misinterpret them). Box 12.2 provides an example of a list of symbols in this case, abbreviations). Like the glossary the list of symbols may be placed before the appendixes or after the table of contents.

THE APPENDIX

An appendix is any section that follows the body of the report and the back matter (i.e. bibliography, glossary and list of symbols). Appendices provide a convenient way to convey information that is too bulky to be presented in the body or that will be of interest to only a small number of the report's readers. For the sake of conciseness, this information is separated from the body of the report. Maps, large technical diagrams or charts, computations, computer printouts, test data and list of supporting documents are usually found in appendices.

Appendices, which are usually lettered rather than numbered (Appendix A, Appendix B, etc.), are listed in the table of contents and referred to at the appropriate points in the body of the report. An item in an appendix is titled 'Appendix'. The item is not called 'Figure' or 'Table' even if it would have been so designated had it appeared in the body of the report.

Before moving on to the next section, read the checklist in Box 12.3. This checklist will help you make sure you have included the appropriate elements in your report and written them correctly.

Box 12.3 Checklist for the Elements of a Report

1. Does the transmittal letter
   a. Clearly state the title and if necessary, the subject and purpose of the report
   b. State who authorized or commissioned the report?
   c. Briefly state the methods you used?
   d. Summarize your major results, conclusions or recommendations?
   e. Acknowledge any assistance you received?
   f. Courteously offer further assistance?
2. Does the title page
   a. Include a title that both suggests the purpose of the report and identifies the type of report?
   b. List the names and positions of both you and your principal reader?
   c. Include the date of submission of the report and any other identifying information?
3. Does the abstract
   a. List your name, the report title and any other identifying information?
   b. Clearly define the problem that led to the project?
   c. Briefly describe (when appropriate) the research methods?
   d. Summarize the major results, conclusions or recommendations?
4. oes the table of contents
   a. Clearly identify the executive summary?
   b. Contain a sufficiently detailed breakdown of the major sections of the body of the report?
   c. Reproduce the headings as they appear in your report?
   d. Include page numbers?
5. Does the list of illustrations (or table or figures) include all of the graphic aids included in the body of the report?

6. Does the executive summary
   a. Clearly state the problem that led to the project?
   b. Explain the major results, conclusions, recommendations and/or managerial implications of your report?
   c. Avoid technical vocabulary and concepts that the managerial audience is not likely to know?
7. Does the glossary include definitions of all the technical terms that your readers might not know?
8. Does your list of symbols include all the symbols and abbreviations that your readers might not know?
9. Do your appendices include the supporting materials that are too bulky to present in the report body or that will interest only a small number of your readers?

THE TEXT OF THE REPORT

The text of a report follows the structure popular in oral presentations:

1. Tell them what you are going to tell (introduction).
2. Tell them (body)
3. Tell them what you told them (summary, conclusions and recommendations)

This kind of structure enables readers to preview and review key points in the report.

Introduction

The introduction of a report

- Contextualizes the report by tying it to a problem or an assignment.
- States the purpose of the report
- Previews the report's contents and organization
- Establishes the tone of the report.

The length of the introduction depends on the length of the report. As a result, the length of the introduction can vary from one or two paragraphs to several pages.

The topics that are generally covered in an introduction are listed below:

- **Authorization.** When how and by whom the report was authorized; who wrote it; and when it was submitted.
- **Problem/purpose.** A statement of what is to be accomplished as a result of the reports.
- **Scope.** What is and what is not going to be covered in the report. The scope indicates the report's complexity.
- **Background.** The factors that have led up to report. This information enables readers to understand how the problem was developed and what has been done about it so far.
- **Limitations.** This section covers the factors affecting the quality of the report, for example, budget and time constraints, unreliability or unavailability of data and so on. Bear in mind, however, that limitations are no excuse for submitting a poor report.
- **Report organization.** The organization of the report along with a rationale for following this plan. This section is a road map that enables readers to anticipate each turn in the report.

Some of these items may be combined in the introduction; and some may not be included at all. You can decide what to include by figuring out what kind of information will help your readers understand and accept your report. Also consider how the introduction relates to the prefatory parts of the report.

However, bear in mind that some people may barely glance at the prefatory parts, so make the introduction detailed enough to provide an adequate preview of the report. If you feel that you need to include information that has already been covered in the prefatory parts, simply use different wordings.

The Body of the Report

This section follows the introduction. It consists of the major sections that present, analyse and interpret the findings gathered as part of your investigation. These sections contain the detailed information necessary to support your conclusions and recommendations.

How much detail should be included? Your decision depends on the nature of your information, the purposes of the report and the preferences of your audience. Some situations call for detailed converge; others can be handled briefly.

A handy rule of thumb to follow: provide only enough detail in the body. Support your conclusions and recommendations and put additional details in tables, charts and appendices.

You also have to decide where to put your conclusions in the body or in a separate section, or both. If the conclusions appear to flow naturally from the evidence, it would be logical to cover them in the body. However, if you want to give your conclusions added emphasis, you may include a separate section to summarize them. Having a separate section is particularly appropriate in longer reports; the reader may lose track of the conclusions if they are given only in the body.

Summary, Conclusions and Recommendations

In a short report this final wrap-up may be only a paragraph or two. A long report generally has separate sections called 'Summary', 'Conclusions' and 'Recommendations'. These three labels differ in that they indicate the following different purposes:

- **Summary.** The key findings of the report, paraphrased from the body and stated (or listed) in the order in which they appear in the body.
- **Conclusions.** This writer's analysis of what the findings mean. In other words, answers to the questions that led to the report.
- **Recommendations.** Opinions, based on reason and logic, about the course of action that should be taken.

If the report is organized deductively, the summary, conclusions and recommendations are presented before the body and are only reviewed briefly at the end. If the report is organized inductively, these sections are presented only at the end and are covered in detail.

The direct (deductive) approach results in a more forceful report, saves the reader's time, and makes the report easy to follow by giving the main idea first. The indirect (inductive) approach helps the writer overcome the reader's resistance by withholding the main idea until later in the report. Because both the direct and indirect approaches recommendations as they go along, rather than putting them either first or last. Business reports are thus often a mix of direct and indirect approaches and cannot be neatly classified by organizational pattern.

Many report writers also combine the conclusions and recommendations under one heading because it is often difficult to present a conclusion without implying a recommendation. Whether you combine them or not, if you have a number of conclusions and recommendations you may want to list them.

In reports that demand action, the recommendation section is particularly important. Readers may fail to take any action if you are vague about what should happen next. You must therefore indicate clearly what is expected of the readers. If possible, include a timetable and a specific course of action.

Notes and Bibliography

When writing the text of the report, decide how to acknowledge your sources. One approach, especially for internal reports, is simply to mention a source in the text. However, this style can be very clumsy, especially when the source requires a fairly long description. Another, more convenient approach, is to cite the source in the text and present the details in the 'note' section at the end of the text of the report. Use Arabic numerals to indicate the appropriate note.

A bibliography is a list of sources consulted when preparing the report. Follow your organization's preferences when structuring the 'note' and 'bibliography'.

THINK ABOUT IT

This chapter covers only the basic framework common to most formal reports. The organization of the text and even the selection and order of the elements of the text will vary with the purpose of the report, the needs of the readers and also the preferences of the organization with which the writer works. Ultimately, it is the total communication context within which the report is being developed that determines the design of the front and back matter (the elements) of the report and the selection and organization of the content of the text of the report.

One of the best ways to learn effective report writing is to examine good reports. This exercise will enable you to see the application of the framework described in this chapter and also the variations that are necessary to accommodate the report writer's subject, purpose and audience.

13

Writing Reports

In this chapter, we will discuss:

- Different Types of Reports
- Four Steps in Writing a Report
- Structuring a Report

DIFFERENT TYPES OF REPORTS

Reports, as mentioned earlier, are business tools. By conveying information objectively from one organizational area to another or from one institution to another, they assist in decision-making and/or problem-solving. Reports are classified into formats; the form, direction, functional use and content of a report are used as the basis for classification. However, a single report might be included to several classifications. The following brief review of classification helps explain the scope or reporting and establishes a departure point for studying reports and reporting.

Formal or Informal Reports

Formal reports are carefully structured; they stress objectivity and organization, contain much detail, and are written in a style that tends to eliminate such elements as personal pronouns. Informal reports are usually short messages with natural, casual use of language. An internal memorandum can generally be described as an informal report.

Short or Long Reports

This is a confusing classification. A one-page memorandum is obviously short, and a twenty-page report is clearly long. But where is the dividing line? Bear in mind that as a report becomes longer (or what you determine as long), it takes on more characteristics of formal reports.

Informational or Analytical Reports

Informational reports (annual reports, monthly financial reports and reports on personnel absenteeism) carry objective information from one area of an organization to another. Analytical reports (scientific research, feasibility reports and real-estate appraisals) present attempts to solve problems.

The Proposal Report

The proposal is a variation of problem-solving reports. A proposal is a document prepared to describe how one organization can meet the needs of another. Most governmental agencies advertise their needs by issuing 'requests for proposal', or RFPs. The RFP specifies a need and potential suppliers prepare proposal reports telling how they can meet that need.

Vertical or Lateral Reports

This classification refers to the direction a report travels. Reports that move upward or downward the hierarchy are referred to as vertical reports, such reports contribute to management control. Lateral reports, on the other hand, assist in coordination in the organization. A report travelling between units of the same organization level (production and finance departments) is lateral.

Internal or External Reports

Internal reports travel within the organization. External reports, such as annual reports of companies, are prepared for distribution outside the organization.

Periodic Reports

Periodic reports are issued on regularly scheduled dates. They are generally upward directed and serve management control. Preprinted forms and computer-generated data contribute to uniformity of periodic reports.

Functional Reports

This classification includes accounting reports, marketing reports, financial reports, and a variety of other reports that take their designation from the ultimate use of the report.

Almost all reports could be included in most of these categories. And a single report could be included in several classifications. Although authorities have not agreed on a universal report classification, these report categories are in common use and provide a nomenclature for the study (and use) of reports.

Reports are also classified on the basis of their format. As you read the classification structure described in the following, bear in mind that it overlaps with the classification pattern described earlier.

FOUR STEPS IN WRITING A REPORT

Writing a report requires careful planning. Although there is great variety in subject matter, audience's needs and types of reports, the following four steps lay the foundation of any report:

1. Defining the problem and the purpose.
2. Identifying and organizing the issues for investigation.
3. Conducting research.
4. Analysing and interpreting data, drawing conclusions and developing recommendations.

The relative importance of these steps varies with the type of assignment. Informational reports, which contain facts alone, may require very little in the way of conclusions and recommendations. Examples of such reports are monitor/control reports and statements of policies and procedures. On the other hand, analytical reports include conclusions and recommendations and require all steps.

Defining the Problem and the Purpose

Research studies often have both a statement of the problem and a statement of the purpose, For example, a real-estate appraiser accepts a client's request to appraise a building to determine its market value. The problem is to arrive at a fair market value for the property. The purpose of the appraisal, however, might be to establish a value for a loan to determine the feasibility of adding to the structure, or to assess the financial possibility of demolishing the structure and erecting something else, the purpose may have to do with determining what elements to consider in arriving at an answer. In other words, unless you know why something is wanted, you might have difficulty knowing what is wanted. Once you arrive at the answer to *why* and *what* questions, you'll be on your way to solving the problem.

Zeroing in on the Problem

To determine the precise nature of the problem, explore your report assignment using the following questions:

- What needs to be determined?
- Why is the issue important?
- Who is involved in the situation?
- Where is the trouble located?
- When did it start?
- How did the situation originate?

These questions are not applicable to all situations, but asking them helps you clarify the boundaries of your investigation. You can then draft a written statement of the problem being investigated, which will serve as a guide to what you are trying to solve or what question you are trying to answer in the report.

If you are writing an analytical report, the problem statement can be broadened: 'Are our salaries competitive and consistent in comparison to the salaries of office support staff in local banks, and how are they affecting service delivery?' This problem statement goes beyond the problem defined earlier because in an analytical report you are expected to look at the facts and, in addition, draw conclusions about the impact of the problem.

Developing the Statement of Purpose

Once you have asked some preliminary questions and determined the problem, you are ready to write a clear statement of purpose that defines the objective of the report. In contrast to the statement of problem, which defines only what you are going to investigate, the statement of purpose defines what the report should accomplish.

In the case of an informational report, you might state your purpose by saying, 'Purpose: To investigate our office support staff salaries to determine whether they are competitive and consistent with salaries of office support staff in local banks'.

However, for an analytical report, your statement of purpose might be, 'Purpose: To identify the differences between the salaries of our office support staff and those of office support staff in other local banks, analyse its effect on service delivery and recommend ways for countering its negative effects'. As you would have observed, problem and purpose statements often have to be combined in one statement. That is why the terms 'problem' and 'purpose' are often used interchangeably. Before you proceed with the report, double-check your statement of purpose with the person who authorized/requested the report.

Identifying Issues for Investigation

Once you have defined the problem and established the purpose of the study you are ready to begin your investigation. To do so, you have to identify the areas that need to be investigated. This can be done by breaking down the 'purpose' into its related aspects.

Of course, the more complex the problem and the purpose, the more the number of areas that need to be investigated. Investigating and solving the problem, however, is only one part of the task, now you have to present it persuasively and clearly to you audience.

STRUCTURING THE REPORT

After the investigation is over, or while it is underway, you have to start structuring your report. Since reports can be structured in a number of ways, you should identify the most suitable structure on the basis of the 'purpose' of your study. This is important because informational assignments are structured differently from analytical ones.

Many assignments require both information and analysis, so it is up to you to determine the overall purpose of your study. Is your general goal to provide background information that someone else will use and interpret? Then an informational outline is suitable, overall; but subsections of the study may require some analysis to discover (and emphasize) important facts. Is the purpose of your study to scrutinize the data and draw your own conclusions and make recommendations? Then use an analytical outline for the report, even though your opinions will be based on facts. For problem-solving you may use a variety of structural schemes, as long as you avoid errors in logical reasoning.

Informational Assignments

Studies that lead to factual reports, offering little scope for analysis or interpretation of data, are generally structured on the basis of subtopics dealing with specific subjects.

These structures are not watertight compartments: a topic organized by category can also be structured by chronology within a larger category. Choose the approach that conveys your subject most clearly, logically and forcefully (but not rudely) to the readers. AQ:2

Analytical Assignments

Analytical studies usually contain analyses, conclusions and recommendations. These studies generally follow a problem-solving method.

Box 13.2: Chronological Pattern

Writing situation to explain to a general audience the geologic history of St. John's, United States Virgin Islands.

1. Introduction
2. Stage One Submarine Volcanism
   a. Logical Evidence: The Pressure Theory
   b. Empirical Evidence: Evidence from ram Head Drillings
3. Stage Two: Above-water Volcanism
   a. Logical Evidence
      - The Role of the Lowered Water Level
      - The Role of Continental Drift
   b. Empirical Evidence: Modern Geological Data
4. Stage Three: Depositing of Organic Marine Sediments
   a. The Role of the Ice Age
      - Water Level
      - Water Temperature
   b. The Role of 'Drowned' Reefs

Source: Markel, Michael H. *Technical Writing: Situations and Strategies.* (New York: St. Martin's Press, 1984).

Hypothesis

When the report's purpose is to discover causes, predict results or suggest a solution to a problem, one way to proceed is to formulate hypothetical explanations. If your problem is to determine why your company is having trouble hiring secretaries, you had better begin analysing this problem by speculating on the reasons. Then after researching the issue, you would organize your report so that you could prove or disprove each reason. You might structure your report like this:

Relative Merit

When the assignment involves evaluation, how well various alternatives meet your criteria, the natural way to structure your analysis is done by focusing on the criteria.

As you would have realized by now, you have to organize your report in the way that best suits your writing situation. These various report structures are only intended ton guide you. Depending on your needs, you might want to blend certain patterns.

One final word of advice regarding the structuring of reports: Structuring can take place simultaneously with the research, or before investigation has commenced, or after the investigation is over. It can also take place during all the three aforementioned stages, constantly being fine-tuned as new information is unearthed. Even after you start writing the report according to the structure you have planned, you may find the need to conduct more investigation to fill in the gaps you discovered while filling out the structure.

CONCLUDING THE REPORT

A 'conclusion' is a logical interpretation of what the facts in your report mean. This interpretation cannot be based on never-before-mentioned information. Whatever conclusions you draw, they must be derived from the facts and information included in your report.

'Recommendations' are inappropriate in a report when you are not expected to supply them, so you must know the difference between 'conclusions' and 'recommendations'. A 'conclusion' is an interpretation of what the facts mean; a 'recommendation' suggests what ought to be done about the facts.

The following is an example of the difference:

Recommendation: 'I recommend that we write a letter to the president offering to buy the company at a 10 per cent premium over the market value of its stock'.

When you have been asked to translate your conclusions into recommendations, make sure that the relationship between them is clear. Keep in mind that your recommendations must be based on logical analysis and sound conclusions. And make sure that your recommendations are detailed clearly so that your readers know exactly what to do with them.

To sum up, report writing involves identifying the problem and purpose, investigating the issue, structuring the material, and ending with conclusions and/or specific recommendations. And at all times, show consideration for the audience. As a regional managing partner at Arthur Anderson and Company says, 'the proposal must be clearly written: very easy to read, free of jargon and buzz words, and to the point!'

THINK ABOUT IT

So now you have a pretty good idea about report writing. First, identify the type of report you have to write; second, identify the problem and purpose of the report; third, investigate the problem and structure the report (be flexible and keep fine-tuning your investigation and report structure). Early on in the process determine whether you will have to write conclusions or recommendations, or both. So when you conduct your investigation you can explore these aspects also.

Now write that report and get that promotion!

14

Managing Data and Using Graphics

In this chapter, we will discuss:

- When to Use Visual Aids
- Selecting a Suitable Visual Aid
- Introducing Visual Aids in the Text

A report's success depends not only on how well you have accessed information through research, but also on how well you have presented it. What techniques can you use to make the data comprehensible? How can you make important points stand out and complex data easy to understand? Your computer can draw any type of image you want, but you have to decide what type of illustration you want and where you want to place it.

WHEN TO USE VISUAL AIDS

To answer the 'when', we have to explore the 'why': why do business professionals use visual aids in reports and presentations?

Visual aids help communicate the subject matter clearly. Imagine reading a paragraph of text describing your company's share of sales and your competitor's share of sales per region. It would be unreadable and incomprehensible. If the same information were tabulated, the information would not only be crystal clear, it would also be easy for the reader to make the necessary comparisons of differences in market share. Visual aids, thus, clarify and simplify data.

Since visual aids tend to get the reader's attention, they also function as attention-getters. As a result, visual aids can also be used to emphasize important material and consequently, to persuade the reader to the writer's point of view.

So when should we use visual aids? When they strengthen our material by clarifying, simplifying or emphasizing it, and when they attract the reader's attention for a specific purpose. Box 14.1 sums up the occasions when we should use visual aids.

As the figure indicates, visual aids can also be used to impress the audience. At the same time, bear in mind that you should not overuse visual aids. Too many visual aids for impressing or attracting the audience might distract your reader and break the continuity of the main argument of your report. At all times, remember that illustrative material only supplements your text, it does not replace it. So put yourself in your reader's shoes and exercise your judgement when using visual aids.

Box 14.1: When to Use Visual Aids

Purpose	Appication
To clarify quantitative composition	Support text descriptions of 'graphic' topics; or numerical information; locations or of an item.
To simplify flowcharts	Break complicated descriptions into components that can be depicted with conceptual models, organization charts or diagrams.
To emphasize	Call attention particularly to important points by illustrating them with line, bar and pie charts.
To summarize	Review major points in the narrative by providing a chart or table that sums up the data.
To reinforce	Present information in visual and written form to increase reader's retention.
To attract	Make material seem more inserting by decorating the cover or title page and by breaking up the text with visual aids.
To impress	Build credibility by putting ideas in visual form to convey the impression of authenticity and precision.
To unify	Depict the relationship among points, for example, with a flowchart.

To determine whether a visual presentation is appropriate and effective, ask yourself the following questions:

- Does the visual presentation contribute to the overall understanding of the subject? Would the visual assist the reader?
- Can the material be covered adequately in words rather than in visual ways? Graphics should be saved for things that are difficult to communicate in words alone.
- Will the written text add meaning to the visual display? (This point will be discussed later in the chapter).
- Is the visual easily understood? Extreme use of colour, complicated symbols, confusing art techniques and unusual combinations of typefaces only detract from the impact of the material presented.

SELECTING A SUITABLE VISUAL AID

In reports, the most commonly used visual aids are tables, bar charts, line charts, pie charts, maps, flowcharts, diagrams and photographs. You should choose the one that best communicates your message to your readers.

Tables

When you have to present detailed, numerical information, use a table, a systematic arrangement of data in columns and rows. Tables are ideal when the audience needs the facts—all the facts—and when the information would be either difficult or clumsy to handle in the main text.

Every table includes vertical columns and horizontal rows, with useful heading along the top and side.

When preparing a numerical table, be sure to identify the units you are expressing: rupees, dollars, percentages, price per kilo, etc. All items in a column are expressed in the same unit.

Bar Charts

The 'simple bar chart' (also called single-range bar chart) is an effective graphic device for quantities. The length of the bar, where they are horizontal or vertical, indicates quantity, as shown in Figure 14.1.

Multiple-range Bar Chart

The 'multiple-range bar chart', also called comparative or cluster bar chart (Figure 14. 2), is useful for expressing data that change over time. The multiple-range bar chart is especially effective in comparing more than one quantity (set of data) at each point along the x-axis, compares the frequency of reported injuries at three plants over an entire year.

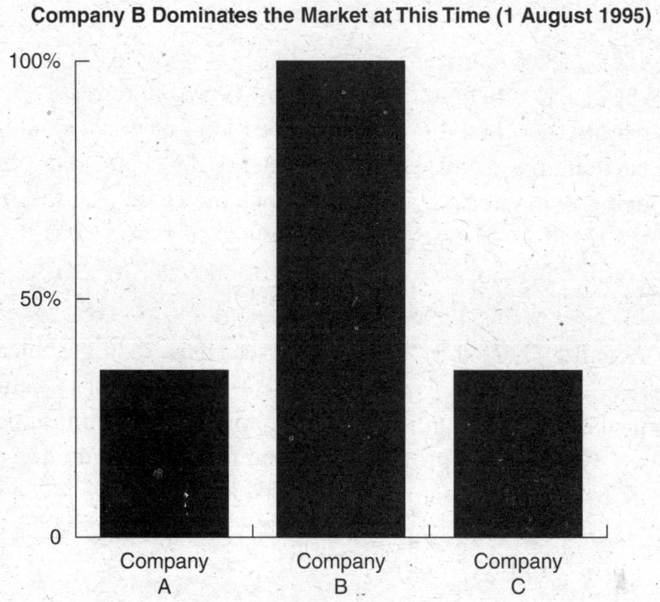

Figure 14.1 **Simple bar chart.**

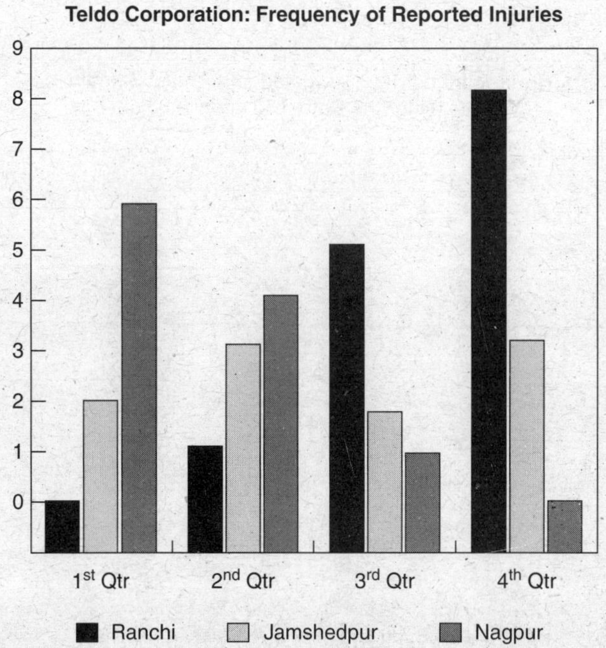

Figure 14.2 **Multiple-range bar chart is useful for comparing more than one quantity over time.**

Stacked-bar Chart

The 'stacked-bar chart', also called component, 100 per cent, or segmented bar chart. When you want to show how different facts (components) contribute to a total figure, the stacked-bar chart is desirable. This graphics is particularly useful when components for more than one-time period are being compared. Figure 14.3 shows the change in the five components of the results of operations over a four-year period.

Gantt Chart

A gantt chart is a horizontal bar chart that graphically displays time relationships. Time is displayed on the horizontal axis and tasks on the vertical axis. This length of the bars depicts the amount of time they represent.

Gantt charts provide a method for determining the sequence and particulars actions that need to be taken to achieve a given objective. In complex operation, they provide managers a useful tool for planning, allocating and scheduling resources.

Line Charts

Line charts, such as the one shown in Figure 14.3, depict changes in quantitative data over time and illustrate trends. Unlike bar charts, which show only the total amount for a time period, line charts show variations within each time period.

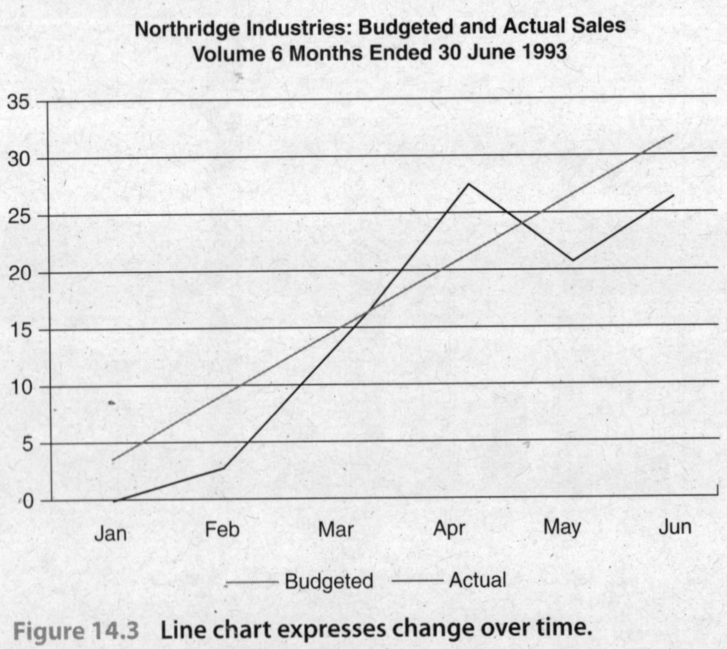

Figure 14.3 Line chart expresses change over time.

When constructing line charts, keep the following general guidelines in mind:

- Use the vertical axis for amount and the horizontal axis for time.
- Begin the vertical axis at zero.
- Divide the vertical and horizontal scales into equal increments. The vertical or amount increments, however, need not be the same as the horizontal or time increments as long as the line or lines drawn will have reasonable slopes. (Unrealistic scales might produce startling slopes that could mislead readers.)

'Area charts', also called cumulative line charts or surface charts, are similar to component bar charts because they show how different factors contribute to the total. The area chart is especially useful when you want to illustrate changes in these components over time. For example, the area chart in Figure 14.4 illustrates the change in the components of a company's capital over a ten-year period. The cumulative total of contributed capital, retained earnings, long-term debt and short-term debt is illustrated by the top line in the chart. The amount of each component can be estimated by visual assessment; labelling the vertical axis on the left and right sides helps the reader estimate amounts. Colours/shading/patterns add visual appeal and aid the reader in distinguishing the components.

Pie Charts

Like stacked-bar charts and area charts, pie charts show how the parts of a whole are distributed. As the name indicates, the whole is represented as a pie, with the parts becoming slices of the pie. Pie charts are effective for

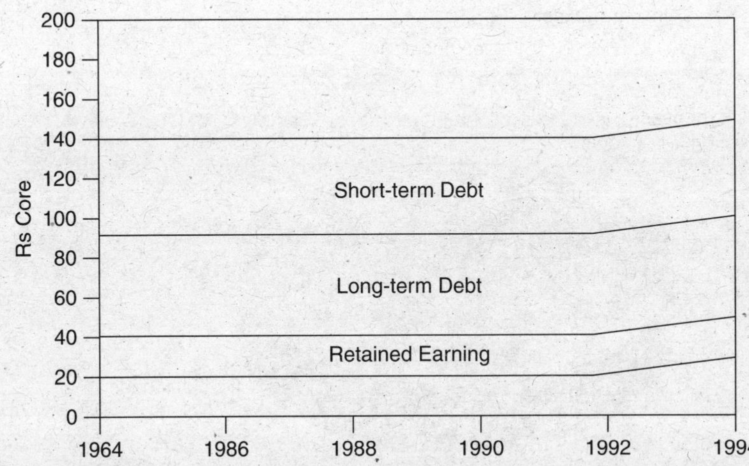

Figure 14.4 Area chart shows how proportional relationship change over time.

showing percentages (parts of a whole), but they are ineffective in showing quantitative totals or comparisons. Bars are used for those purposes.

The pie chart in Figure 14.5 illustrates the information reported on a company's income statement. The pie depicts sales; the slices represent various types of expenses.

Following are some generally used guidelines for constructing pie charts:

1. Position the largest slice to be emphasized at the 12 o'clock position. Working clockwise, place the other slices in descending order of the size or some other logical order of presentation. (Unfortunately, some software programmes will not allow you to organize the slices in the way you want.)
2. Label each slice and include information about the quantitative size (percentage, dollars, rupees, square feet, etc.) of each slice.
3. Draw attention to one more slices if you wish by
   (a) exploding the slices(s) to be emphasized, (i.e. removing it from immediate contact with the pie) or
   (b) displaying and printing on the slice(s) to be emphasized. When exploding a slice, place it in such a way that it does not intrudes into the title.
4. Use colour or patterns to help the reader differentiate among the slices and to add to appeal.

For dramatic effect, many periodicals and reports vary from these general rules. So use your own judgement when constructing a pie chart.

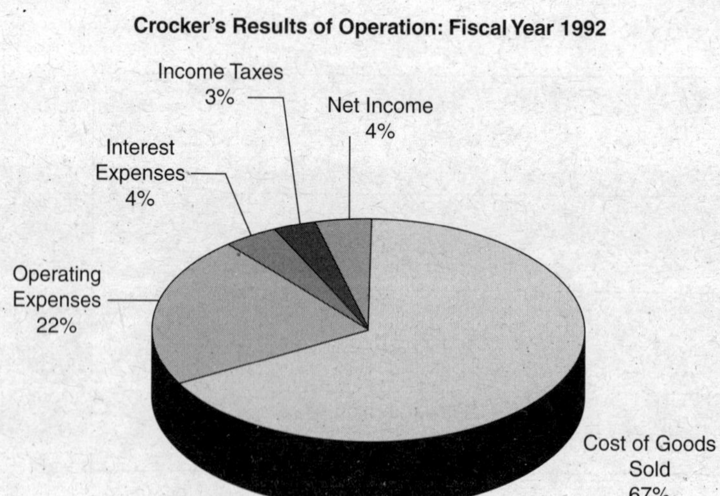

Figure 14.5 Pie chart with three-dimensional effect shows percentages of a whole.

Pictograms

A pictogram uses pictures to illustrate numerical relationship. For example, in place of a simple bar chart, coins can be used instead of bars to depict additions to personal savings. However, pictograms can be more dramatic than meaningful if they are not planned properly. For example, doubling the height and width of a picture increases the total area four times. Care must be taken to ensure that all symbols are of the same size so that true relationships are not distorted.

Maps

Maps help readers visualize geographic relationships and are especially useful when the reader may not be familiar with the geography discussed. A map can, for example, effectively present sales growth by state and show the location of the home office, distribution centres and retail stores within the geographic region. By giving the information visually, a map eliminates the difficulty of explaining the information in words. In addition to being less confusing, a map is also more concise and interesting than a written message.

Flowcharts and Organization Charts

If you need to show physical or conceptual relationships rather than numerical ones, you might want to use a flowchart or an organization chart. Flowcharts are indispensable when illustrating processes, procedures and relationships. A health centre administrator can easily explain the processing of clients through the flowchart in Figure 14.6.

An organization chart illustrates the positions, units, or functions of an organization and the way they interrelate. An organization's normal communication channels are almost impossible to describe without the help of a chart like the one in Figure 14.7.

Other Visual Aids

Floor plans, photographs, diagrams, cartoons, blueprints and lists of various sorts may be included in reports. The increased availability of graphics and sophisticated drawing software leads to their inclusion in reports and oral presentations. Because managers can quickly prepare these visuals themselves, these sophisticated graphics are being used increasingly for internal reports.

Frequently, you will have some material that must be included in the report, but would make the discussion/argument unwieldy. In this case, the material might be placed in an appendix and only referred to in the report.

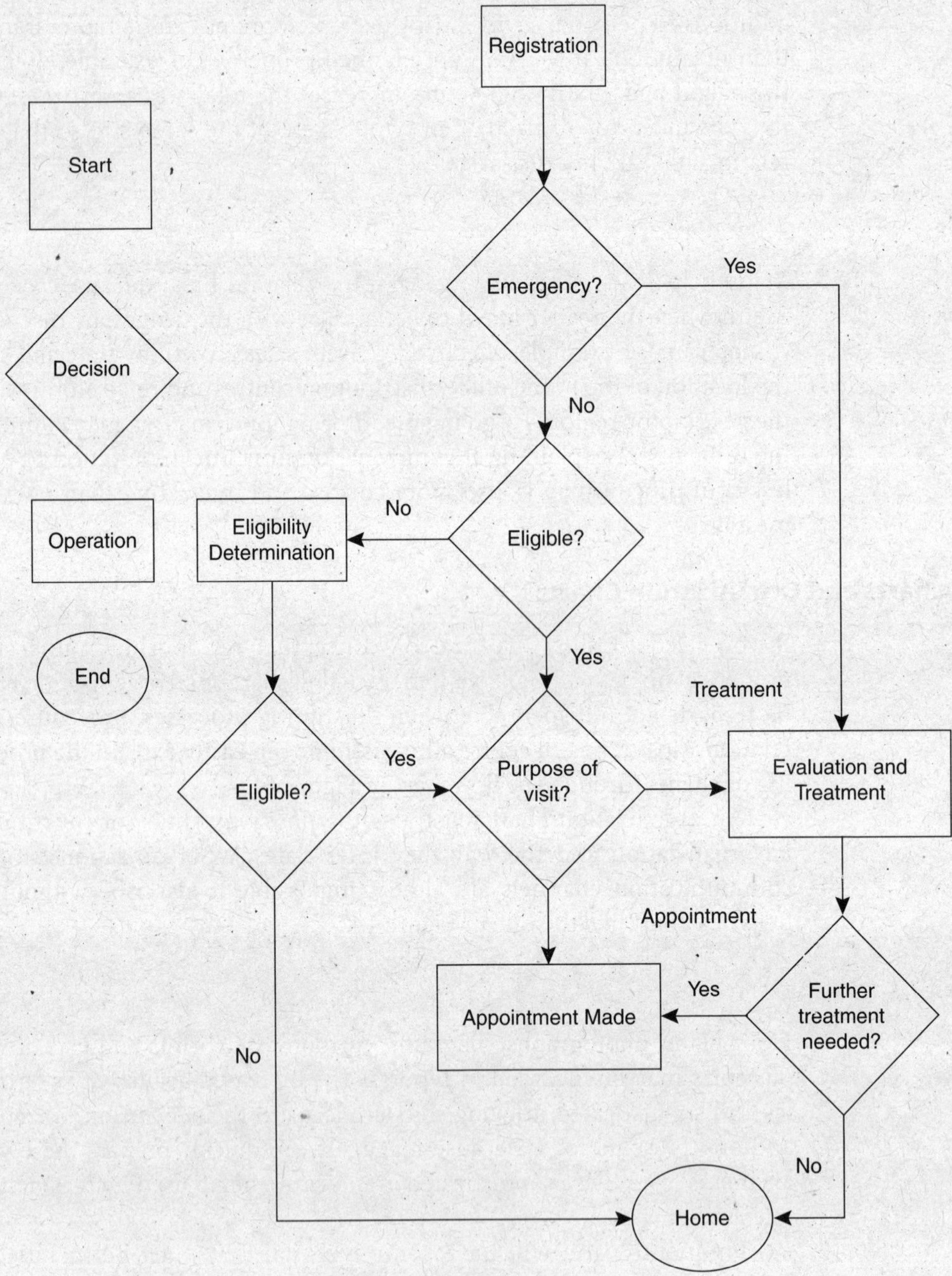

Figure 14.6 Flow of clients through health centre.

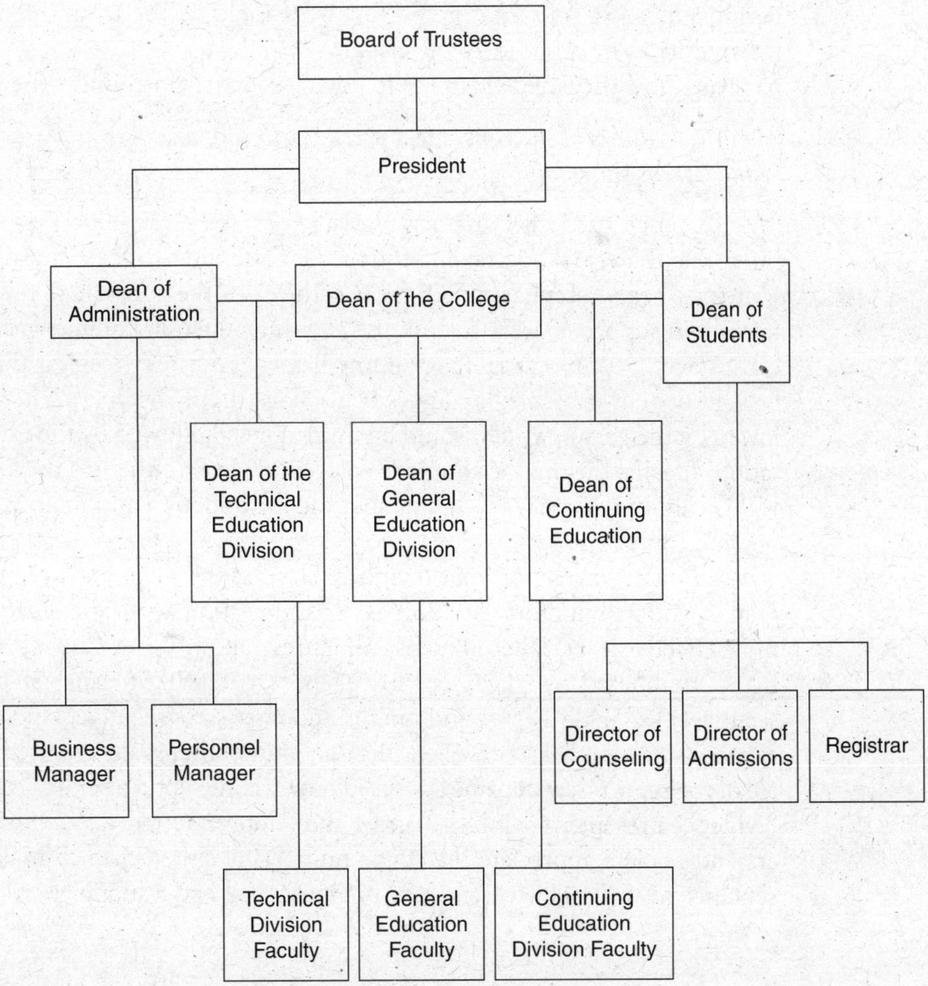

Figure 14.7 Flow of clients through health centre.

INTRODUCING VISUAL AIDS IN THE TEXT

As mentioned earlier in the chapter, the visual aids supplement the text, and the text adds meaning to the visual aid. The text and the visuals are partners in the communication process. Under no conditions should a visual be included in the report without being referred to in the textual material. If readers come across illustrations in the text before they have been told about them, they will draw their own inferences and conclusions from the visual. But if they have been informed about the visual and its implications, the visual will supplement what has been said. In addition, the text can direct the reader's attention to that aspect of the illustration that the writer wishes to make a special mention of. In other words, visual aids have to be introduced to and interpreted for the readers by the text. This is also referred to as 'integration' of the visual within the text.

Note how the language in the following sentence introduces the visual:

About two-thirds of the consumers preferred to shop in suburban areas than in the city, as shown in Figure 1.

This sentence uses introductory phrasing: 'as shown in Figure 1'. It also interprets the visual by drawing the reader's attention to the point that the writer wishes to emphasize: 'About two-thirds of the consumers preferred to shop in suburban areas than in the city'. Introduction and interpretation can be achieved in one sentence immediately above the visual or they can be split up. For example, the figure could have simply been introduced followed by the graph, which would be immediately followed by the interpretation. Ideally, the 'figure' should be placed as close to the text as possible. If this cannot be achieved, do not split the introduction and interpretation portions of the text.

Although your report may include tables, graphs, maps and even photographs, you will find organization easier and writing about the illustrations more effective if you label all items as 'Figures' followed by a number and the figures numbered in serial order. Some report writers like to label tables consecutively as 'Table 1', etc., and graphs and charts consecutively in another sequence as 'Graph 1', etc. When this dual numbering system is used, readers of the report may become confused if they come upon a sentence saying, 'Evidence presented in Tables 3 and 4 and Graph 2 supports ....' Both writers and readers appreciate the single numbering system, which makes the sentence read, 'Evidence presented in Figures 3, 4 and 5 supports...'

15

Caselets and Questions

PART A: CASELETS

Caselet 1

A

Your boss has been telling of late that he would welcome suggestions about how to improve the organization. You take him at his word and end up meeting him to discuss some of your ideas with him. As you begin to outline the changes you propose, he fixes you with a stare and folds his arms across his chest; as you go on, the frown on his face gathers intensity. When you finish, he gets up abruptly and says, with barely suppressed menace in his voice, 'Thank you very much. Your ideas are priceless'.

B

Your friend has started a new organization. He is encountering some labour problems. You are a personnel management specialist and have several years of experience in the personnel department of a large conglomerate. Your friend calls you over to his office one day to discuss his problems. He finds your ideas innovative and thinks they are just right for his kind of set up. as you get up to leave, your friend clasps your head warmly, beams at you and says, 'Thank you very much. Your ideas are priceless'.

Questions for Discussion

1. Verbally the two messages are exactly the same. Do you think the two speakers were communicating the same message?
2. What is it that makes the two messages so different?

Caselet 2

DATE: 2 December 2000

TO: Shirin Lakdawalla
FROM: Bairam Pestonjee

SUBJECT: Improving Communication with our overseas suppliers

The intercultural concepts that were discussed at the most recent managerial convocation lead me to believe that it would behove you to investigate the causal factors that account for these differences and to determine how we might capitalize on these findings through a detailed analysis of our international management agreements with our overseas suppliers and concessionaries.

Questions for Discussion

1. Bairam Pestonjee seems to have swallowed a dictionary. In spite of the excellent vocabulary, the memo does not convey its point effectively. Why?
2. Make an attempt to understand the memo and rewrite it effectively.

Caselet 3

Shireen Dastoor is Director of Marketing and New Product Development for Make Believe Software Inc. At a recent meeting, the board of directors decided to eliminate an entire line of games software and replace it with a line of education software. This would mean much reassigning between each department.

Shireen immediately scheduled a half-day meeting with her market researchers and project managers. At the meeting, Shireen introduced her staff to the need for refocusing development efforts and explained which projects should now receive the department's emphasis. Then she said, 'I would like all of you to continue working together today to develop a proposal outlining which teams will handle which projects. Then I would like to meet with you again to review the proposal in case I have any questions or concerns.

The next day, Shireen and her staff met to review the proposal. She found that they had not only made a sound division of labour, but had also suggested some ways to co-team on certain projects to move them along more quickly. In addition, the group identified two critical questions for Shireen to take up with the board.

Questions for Discussion:

1. What effect did Shireen's including her staff in decision-making have on the members of her work team? What effect might it have on the board's decisions?
2. Describe a more authoritarian, 'top-down' way Shireen might have used to handle the situation? What would the result have been?

Caselet 4

The weekly budget meetings at Fast Paced Productions was a 'routing' meeting every week same day, time, place and participants. Pavan Kumar made it a habit to arrive at 10 minutes late every day.

On Fridays, Pavan walked in, Sharada Pawar, a co-worker, noticed that Harish Awara, who had been speaking to the group, sneered momentarily before turning back to the board and continued with his presentation.

At lunch, Sharada joined Pavan in the cafeteria. 'That was some look you got from Harish this morning', she remarked. 'You noticed that too, huh?' replied Pavan. 'What is his problem?' 'Well you were late'. Sharada pointed out. Impatient, Pavan responded, 'Sharada, you know all those meetings start out with the same old thing. Harish gives a ten-minute play-by-play that we could read off the budget sheet in 30 seconds!'

'But Pavan', Sharada continued. 'You would not be late for a meeting with Raj, would you?' 'Of course not!' exclaimed Pavan. 'He is the president of the company. I would never keep him waiting. It would not be professional or political!' Sharada raised her eyebrows. 'But you think it is okay to keep your co-workers waiting?'

'Now wait, Sharada that is not fair', Pavan objected.

'You know I think the budget meetings are important'.

Questions for Discussion

1. What does not Pavan understand?
2. What message is he sending by coming late to budget meetings?
3. What could happen as a result of his behaviour?

Caselet 5

Hrithik Roshan was a scientist in the environmental lab of a chemical processing plant, Petunia chemicals. He was asked by the town council to explain the company's pollution reduction activities and how these efforts conform to local, state and national regulations. The council called on Hrithik because he was known as an authority on the subject of pollution control.

Hrithik was very comfortable with his topic, so he readily outlined the information he would cover in his talk. Because he was rarely called on to speak in public, he decided to write his presentation in full. Here is an excerpt:

> With regard to national regulations, I will, if you please, expound upon the exemplary record of Petunia chemicals. No other company of similar size or stature has maintained the stringent effluent regulatory standards that are the hallmark of Petunia Chemicals' environmental policy. The polemic of certain strident environmental groups aside, we at Petunia Chemicals do care deeply about preserving our each and our future on this planet.

Questions for Discussion

1. How do you think Hrithik's speech was received by the town council?
2. Why do you think Hrithik chose to speak in this style?
3. What constructive criticism would you give him?

Caselet 6

At a press conference, Tomal Mukherjee, the press secretary for a large IT company is taking questions about the company's downsizing. Barkha Dutt, a reporter shouts her question: 'Mr. Mukherjee, is there any chance the company will lay off the additional employees within the next year?' 'As I said earlier', Mr. Mukherjee replied, 'we have been studying our operations very closely nationwide in an effort to be sure that we are doing all that we can to keep layoffs to a minimum. At this point, we accept the next quarter to turn sales around as some of our subsidiary divisions get up and running. That is the last question, folks. Thank you for your time'.

Scribbling furiously, Barkha ran to the phone to call in her story before her deadline. Barkha's story began. 'Keypad Systems plans no more layoffs in the coming year, according to spokesperson Tomal Mukherjee'.

Later the same day, Barkha's editor was furious to see a front-page story in a rival paper where the reporter had presented the story quite differently. The rival story began, 'Are more layoffs in store at Keypad Systems? At a press conference today, company spokesperson Tomal Mukherjee skirted the question, leaving hundreds of employees and subscontractors hanging in the balance'

Questions for Discussion

1. Why might the two stories have been different?
2. Did Tomal Mukherjee answer Barkha's question?
3. Whose information was correct, Barkha's or the other reporter's?

Caselet 7

Amar Patrikas purchased a photocopier from Deluxe Products for his employer's graphic design business. Amar traded the old copier in because it kept breaking down; the repairs were expensive and inconvenient. With this in mind Harbinder Ahuja, the Deluxe sales representative says to Amar, 'This service and maintenance contract covers you for a full year. If anything goes wrong with the copier just pick up the phone and we will be over in no time at all plus the maintenance schedule keeps the machine in optimum shape',

Amar thought about it only briefly. He knew how important it was to have a reliable copier. 'That sounds great, Harbinder'. He said. 'Where do I sign?'

A few days later, the bill for the copier and service contract arrived. Amar's boss, the owner of the company, called him in to discuss it. 'Amar', he began, 'I'm a little surprised by the bottom line on this copier deal. Why did you agree to a service and maintenance contract? Is there some reason this new state-of-the-art machine should not be reliable?'

Questions for Discussion

1. Why do you think Amar was so quick to sign the agreement?
2. What are some things he should have thought about? What questions should he have asked?
3. How did not thinking critically about the sales representative's pitch affect Amar and his company?

Caselet 8

Date: 20 October 2000

To: Avinash Kumar
From: Mamata Banerjee

Subject: Purchase of New Computers

As per your express commandments, I have placed an order for the purchase of 20 new Pentium III systems, with Santosh electronics. Mr. Santosh who owns this outfit, was needless to say, delighted at the order, and has invited me to lunch with him to celebrate the deal. Perhaps you can also join us, if you please.

Questions for Discussion

1. What is wrong with this memo?
2. Rewrite the memo, cutting out all redundant words phrases and making it clear and concise.

Caselet 9

1. Answers will vary, broadly, the following points should be covered

   Mr. Blunderbuzz

   Came late (took the audience for granted);

   Did not establish eye contact with the audience;

   Started speech with verbal segregates (er, uh) indicating lack of confidence, perhaps lack of preparation;

2. Answers will vary. Basically, the student is expected to discuss the nonverbal aspects of his presentation and suggest ways in which he can improve his nonverbal skills.

Caselet 10

1. This memo will have a demoralizing and devastating effect on the reader. He will probably be less instead of more confident at his next presentation. As a result, he will probably make a worse presentation. It is highly unlikely that in this frame of mind he will ask the help of the training consultant (even the writer does not seem confident that the training consultant would be able to help)

   The employee might be too demotivated by this memo to put it any effort in any future project that is assigned to him.

2. The memo and a commentary on its drawbacks are given as follows:

   12 June 2000
   Amar Patnaik

   [1] *SUBSTANDARD PERFORMANCE*

   [2] *Your presentation to Josh Company representatives this morning was below our standards.*

   [3] *The following weaknesses were apparent:*

   1. *Too technical*
   2. *Participants had no chance for hands-on experience.*
   3. *Failure to get participants to respond to questions for fear that they would look foolish*

   [4] *I insist that the presentation be revised before the same firm sends another group of representatives to visit us next week*

   [5] *You might check to see whether our training consultant can be helpful.*

   Anjali Joshi

   Marketing Manager

Commentary

1. As a subject line, these words immediately put the reader on the defensive.
2. Emphasizes a negative thought by placing it in the first sentence and using negative language.
3. Emphasizes negatives with negative words (*weakness* and *failure*). Emphasizes unpleasant points by using tabulation and enumeration.
4. Seems unnecessarily demanding ('I insist').
5. Unnecessarily weak in referring to action ('You might check').

Caselet 11

1. Answers will vary broadly, the following points should be covered:
   a. The supervisor is too preoccupied with her own problems to listen to Usha's problems;
   b. She talks too much and gives strong nonverbal signals that she is not interested in what Usha has to say.
2. The supervisor's attitude is likely to have demoralized and discour aged Usha. She may never approach Alka again with her problems.
3. Answers will vary.

Caselet 12

1. The irrelevant questions:

   Do I come from a family of Nobel laureates?

   Do they require tall people for this job?

   What are the genetic requirements?

   What handicaps are considered prerequisite?

   Can I get kickbacks?

   What are the imaginary rewards?

   Is the field affected by heat and cold?

   Will the field be strongly influenced by changes in the earth's magnetic field?

   Is confrontation in the field increasing?
2. Answers will vary. Any relevant question is acceptable.

Caselet 13

A

1. Ajith did not have the desirable qualification
2. He spoke in a very casual and crude manner
3. His lack of knowledge about the company shows his indifference towards the job.
4. He is clearly only interested only in the salary.
5. He is very 'I' centred.

B

If Ajith was really interested in a career in sales, he should have taken the opportunity while in college to gain practical experience. He could have done this by taking more courses in marketing and sales, finding a part-time sales position, or doing an internship for a local company. All of this would have made him a more attractive candidate to the interviewer.

Caselet 14

1. The memo does not convey its point effectively because:
   a. It uses words that the reader is not likely to understand.
   b. The sentences are too long to follow.
   c. The writer does not get to the point immediately.
2. The memo can be rewritten as follows

   DATE: 2 *December 2000*
   TO: *Shirin Lakdawalla*
   FROM: *Bairam Pestonjee*

   SUBJECT: *Improving Communication with our Overseas Suppliers.*

   As a result of our recent management meeting, I think an evaluation of all contracts with our overseas suppliers and concessionaires is in order. I would like you to find out what can be done to improve our relationships with these people. Please send me your ideas as soon as possible.

Caselet 15

The writer's attitude appears too casual. Instead of being reader-oriented she is very writer-oriented, always talking about herself instead of explaining how she can meet the needs of the organization.

Not only is her language too casual, it is also ungrammatical. The letter also contains a spelling mistake. 'Passified' should have been 'pacified'. In any case, this word is not suitable in this context. The 'r' in research should be capitalized.

The letter only repeats the contents of the resume. It talks about her qualification but does not demonstrate her abilities and what she can do for the organization. Her reference to her work experience does not show how it would be relevant for the post she is applying for. The letter reveals nothing positive about her personality or her ability to work effectively in the Institute of Chartered Financial Analysis of India as a Research Associate.

Caselet 16

A

1. The letter merely presents information that would be readily available in the resume.
2. The writer merely mentions his work experience, but does not show how it makes him more suitable for the job he is applying for
3. The writer makes broad statements of his ability and does not support them with proof.

Overall, the letter is very writer-centred and does not reveal the writer's abilities, personality, or 'fit' with position he is applying for.

B

1. Because of the clichéd opening and conclusion
2. Because it is writer-centred instead of audience-oriented
3. Because it does not provide a vivid description of the writer's personality or abilities.

Caselet 17

This is not an effective contents page. Because it is all in caps all headings are given equal importance. In a well-written contents page, a reader can comprehend the argument by reading the headings alone. But the headings in this contents page do not indicate what is being analysed and do not reveal what the writer considers better or more rewarding. All the pages are not covered in this contents page, thus making it difficult for the reader to locate particular items. Perhaps the writer has not made enough subheadings.

Caselet 18

This is not an effective contents page. All headings are given equal importance, though the indentation does help differentiate them. In a well-written contents page, a reader can comprehend the argument by reading the headings alone. But the headings in this contents page do not indicate what is being analysed, what the committees do or whether the 'additional considerations' are obstacles or advantages. Except for page 6 all the pages are covered, thus enabling the writer to locate particular items.

Caselet 19

An executive summary should be precise and geared to meet the needs of managers. This is not a good summary.

1. It is too long.
2. It discusses technical matters that managers are not concerned with.
3. It barely addresses managerial concerns about 'implementation.' After all, it is the managers who will have to implement this pay plan.

Caselet 20

1. The job application letter is not well-written. Although answers will vary, they must cover tone, content, choice of words and the writer's attitude.
2. *Dear Ms. Parikh,*

   Your advertisement in the January 31 issue of the Chapel Hill Post attracted my attention because I believe that I have the 'proven skills' you are looking for in an administrative assistant. In addition to having previous experience in a variety of office settings, I am familiar with the computer system that you use in your office.

   I recently completed a three-course sequence at St. Xavier's College on operation of the Beta Computer System. I learned how to apply this technology to speed up letter-writing and report-writing tasks. A workshop on 'Writing and Editing with the Beta Processor' gave me edge over other valuable applications.

   As a result of this training, I am able to compose many types of finished documents, including sales letters, financial reports and presentation slides.

   These specialized skills have proven valuable in any work for the past 8 months as assistant to the chief nutritionist at the University of Kolkata campus cafeteria. As my resume indicates, my duties include drafting letters, typing finished correspondence and handling phone calls. I am particularly proud of the order-confirmation system, I designed, which has sharply reduced the problem of late shipments and depleted inventories.

   Because 'proven skills' are next explained in person, I would appreciate an interview with you. Please phone me any afternoon between 3 and 5 p.m. at 8675432 to let me know the day and time most convenient for you.

   Sincerely

   Tarun Ghosh

   Enclosure

Caselet 21

1. Raj Ganeshan should not antagonize his readers over such a minor issue. He should tone down his aggressive and abusive style and state his request firmly and politely. Since everyone obviously does need the copier he should arrive at a compromise solution.
2. The memo can be rewritten as follows

   To: All employees
   From: Raj Ganeshan, General Manager

   Sub: Use of Copiers

   We are revamping our policy on the use of copiers for personal matters. In the past, we have not encouraged personnel to use them for such purposes because of the costs involved. But we also recognize, perhaps belatedly, that we can solve the problem if each of us pays for what he takes.

   We are therefore putting these copiers on a pay-as-you-go basis. The details are simple enough and will be posted on the copiers.

Caselet 22

1. Anita failed to understand Jatin's needs. She made a sales pitch that confused and intimidated Jatin.
2. She should have first encouraged Jatin to speak, before she decided what she needed. Her sales pitch should not have been full of technicalities.
3. Anita lost the customer and the company lost good will.
4. Jatin was confused, intimidated and driven to seek help elsewhere.

Caselet 23

1. As there is little two-way communication between Ranjit and the editors, he is unaware of the unhappiness caused by his decision to assign all the workshops to Vijaya. If he had not learned about the general discontent from the grapevine, there would have been growing discontent among the editors and the quality of work would have suffered.
2. Vijaya did not help matters by not communicating her resentment to Ranjit. Had she been more forthcoming, the communication problems could have been avoided.

Caselet 24

1. Shireen's democratic approach motivated the group to put in the best and make suggestions freely. For the board, the questions raised by the researchers and project managers comprised valuable feedback that they could use while making failure decisions.
2. Answers will vary. They must be logically developed.

Caselet 25

1. Pavan does not understand that his co-workers deserve to be treated with more respect and that he is only making things difficult for himself by not being courteous to them.
2. By coming late to the budget meetings, Pavan is showing his lack of interest and his cavalier attitude to his colleagues.
3. Answers will vary.

Caselet 26

1. Meenakshi clearly did not listen to Ranjan. She interrupted him and spoke to him in a dismissive manner. She was unable to recall what Ranjan had said at the last meeting. Most probably she had not even registered his grievances.
2. Answers will vary.

Caselet 27

1. Answers will vary. Broadly, the answer must touch upon the incomprehensibility of the speech.
2. Answers will vary.
3. Answers will vary.

Caselet 28

1. Arundhati's anecdote was successful because:
   a. it was suitable
   b. it was humorous
   c. it was inoffensive
   d. it put the audience in a receptive frame of mind.

   As the audience was already sceptical, lecturing to them would have only made them more defensive.
2. Answers will vary.

Caselet 29

1. Tomal Mukherjee did not answer Barkha's question in a direct manner. Barkha did not listen carefully to what Tomal had said. Unlike the other reporter, she did not use the implications of what he had said.
2. Though Tomal did answer Barkha's question, he did so in a rather roundabout way.
3. The other reporter's information was correct.

Caselet 30

1. The urgent need for a reliable copier and the successful sales pitch made by the salesman spurred Amar to sign the agreement without giving it much thought.
2. He should have asked the salesman the same questions that his boss asked him.
3. Amar's hasty decision resulted in unnecessary expenses for the company and caused Amar considerable embarrassment.

Caselet 31

1. The information in this resume is arranged chronologically.
2. Answers will vary. The student is expected to present a logical argument for or against the chronological arrangement.

Caselet 32

1. **Personal details:** Most of the personal details such as those on health, father's name, father's age, father's occupation, nationality, etc. are redundant. Special hobbies should be more productive or creative.
2. **Education:** Words like 'scrape through' have a negative connotation. It could be replaced by something like 'with 80 per cent marks in Math and English' or something; +2 details need not be mentioned. The 86th rank in the university is nothing to write home about. It is best left out.
3. The resume can be rewritten by weeding out all the unnecessary details mentioned above and by including more relevant information.

Caselet 33

1. Answers will vary. Broadly, the answer must touch upon the writer's tone, choice of works, verbosity and tendency to include irrelevant information and the omission of the designation of the sender and the receiver in the memo.
2. The memo may be suitably rewritten, by avoiding the drawbacks that are so evident in the original version.

PART B—MULTIPLE CHOICE QUESTIONS

1. Nonverbal messages can communicate all of the following except
   a. anger
   b. ideas
   c. distrust
   d. scepticism
2. Voice qualities include all of the following except
   a. volume
   b. gestures
   c. rate of speech
   d. pronunciation
3. Maintaining eye contact is generally perceived as an indication of
   a. honesty
   b. ruthlessness
   c. sadness
   d. happiness
4. Proxemics is the study of how people use the ____________ around them:
   a. colour schemes
   b. sound levels
   c. physical space
   d. emotional storms
5. The ____________within a radius of about 18 inches around a person is reserved for close relations and friends:
   a. personal distance
   b. personal stance
   c. personal standing
   d. personal status
6. The study of nonverbal signals is divided into three areas: paralanguage, proxemics and ________
   a. kinesics
   b. kinetics
   c. kinship
   d. none of the above

7. Four common gestures are
   a. emblems, adaptors, regulators, illustrators
   b. embellishments, adaptors, regulators, illustrators
   c. emblems, adaptives, regulators, illustrators
   d. emblems, adaptors, regulations, illustrators
8. Audible sounds like sighing, laughing and groaning are called
   a. vivacious characteristics
   b. vital characteristics
   c. vicious characteristics
   d. vocal characteristic
9. To listen means to get _________ from what is heard
   a. mean
   b. mileage
   c. meaning
   d. meanness
10. Which of the following best describes these hindrances to effective listening: distracting sounds, poor acoustics and uncomfortable seating arrangements?
    a. attitudinal barriers
    b. environmental barriers
    c. ecological barriers
    d. biological barriers
11. Which of these sentences sum up the attitude of a listener who is overly concerned with himself?
    (i) I must defend my position
    (ii) I already know what you have to say
    (iii) Am I coming too strong?
       a. Only 1
       b. Only 2
       c. 2 and 1
       d. 1, 2 and 3
12. A person trying to understand a speaker's message in totality, to interpret the meaning as precisely as possible, is engaged in _________ listening.
    a. comprehensive
    b. composite

c. complicated
d. convex

13. Which of the following strategies does not help you to listen better?
    a. being alert to all cues
    b. being prepared to listen
    c. faking attention
    d. resisting distractions

14. __________listening entails a conscious effort to keep one's emotions and prejudices at bay.
    a. objective
    b. biased
    c. advanced
    d. premature

15. Which of these techniques will not help a speaker to encourage effective listening among his audience?
    a. adjusting delivery
    b. utilizing feedback
    c. rambling aimlessly
    d. being lucid

16. Team-oriented relationships are marked by
    (i) cooperation
    (ii) honesty
    (iii) mutual disrespect
        a. 1 and 2
        b. 3
        c. 2 and 3
        d. None of the above

17. A supervisor who tells his sub ordinate. 'Do it this way because I am the boss and I say so', is likely to
    a. jeopardize his own life
    b. antagonize the subordinate
    c. endear himself to the subordinate
    d. motivate the subordinate to work harder

18. A __________message is one in which the speaker attempts to manipulate or coerce the listener.
    a. controlling
    b. contemptuous

c. convoluted
d. contentious

19. As a critic, you can ensure that your comments meet with the least resistance by doing all of the following except
    a. understanding the other person's perspective
    b. sounding judgmental
    c. avoiding critical overload
    d. directing criticism at the person's behaviour, not at the person
20. In which of these cases is it advisable to avoid a direct confrontation in a conflict situation?
    a. when you are anxious to go on a holiday
    b. when you perceive that you have no chance of satisfying your concerns
    c. when it is not advisable to allow emotions to settle
    d. when you do not need time to gather facts or think about a situation
21. In a compromising approach to conflict resolution cooperation between the two parties, it is dictated by
    a. jealousy
    b. altruism
    c. self-interest
    d. good manners
22. Which of these is not a strategy for defusing and redefining a conflict?
    a. make sure everyone hears the same message
    b. separate the main issue from personal feelings
    c. settle for nothing less than 100 per cent
    d. allow for cool down time before resolution
23. In today's business world, the success of an organization to a great extent depend on whether the workforce has the necessity to establish a positive work environment
    a. risk-taking abilities
    b. interpersonal skills
    c. childishness
    d. cleverness
24. A win–lose approach to negotiation is marked by ________ and may create ill will.
    a. savagery
    b. harmony

c. competitiveness

d. laziness

25. A lose–lose approach to negotiation is adopted when the negotiating partners
    a. want to hurt each other
    b. want to win each other's trust
    c. are willing to consider each other's needs
    d. are desperate to find an acceptable solution
26. Two division heads want a full-time secretary each but budget restrictions make this impossible. Eventually, they agree to share one secretary. This is an example of
    a. win–win approach
    b. a compromise
    c. a lose–lose approach
    d. a win–lose approach
27. Which of these actions do not facilitate a win–win approach?
    a. determining the needs of both parties
    b. developing a list of possible solutions
    c. choosing the most appropriate solution
    d. forcing the other party to accept your views
28. To negotiate skillfully you must have knowledge of all the variables and their possible use as
    a. contortions
    b. concessions
    c. confessions
    d. conclusions
29. Which of the following does not help the negotiating parties to reach an acceptable agreement?
    a. identifying one's priorities and needs beforehand
    b. keeping one's emotions in check
    c. responding to personal attacks
    d. listening actively and keeping an open mind
30. Negotiating cannot be learned by following a prepackaged set of principles because
    a. people are not always rational or predictable
    b. people are often dictatorial or not
    c. people are not often superstitious
    d. people are not always punctual

31. Which of these is not a business interview?
    (i) Employment interview
    (ii) Performance appraisal interview
    (iii) Disciplinary interview
    a. 1 and 2
    b. 1 and 3
    c. 2 and 3
    d. None of the above
32. Which of these is not a problem that calls for disciplinary action?
    a. chronic absenteeism
    b. insubordination
    c. family problems
    d. disobedience
33. In a _______ interview, the interviewer takes almost complete charge of the flow of conversation by asking specific questions.
    a. non-directive
    b. directive
    c. jocular
    d. random
34. 'Are you familiar with our policy on absenteeism?' This question is an example of
    a. a close-ended question
    b. a dubious question
    c. a harsh question
    d. an open question
35. Which of these is a hypothetical question?
    a. if I were to introduce five-day weeks, do you think the staff would be happy?
    b. if you knew you could not do the work, why did you take up the responsibility?
    c. are you satisfied with my leadership?
    d. why are you always late to office?
36. If an interviewer wants to take notes he must do so
    a. aggressively
    b. unobtrusively
    c. hastily
    d. egregiously

37. Which of these is an ethical guideline for an interviewer?
    a. make unrealistic promises
    b. reveal confidential information
    c. ask illegal questions
    d. none of the above
38. Interviewers should conduct themselves in a ______manner and avoid being overly friendly or familiar with the respondent.
    a. colloquial
    b. professorial
    c. professional
    d. loquacious
39. Which of these is not a factor that affects group dynamics?
    a. size of the group
    b. leadership
    c. status of different members
    d. none of the above
40. In group problem-solving, the _______stage, is the stage when members disagree with each other and debate ideas.
    a. orientation
    b. emergence
    c. conflict
    d. reinforcement
41. Reflective thinking involves which of these steps?
    (i) Problem identification
    (ii) Problem generation
    (iii) Solution evaluation
        a. 1 and 2
        b. 1 and 3
        c. 1
        d. 2 and 3
42. Which of these is not a question that the convener must consider when he is planning a meeting?
    a. Why have a meeting?
    b. What type of meeting is called for?
    c. Where should the meeting be held?
    d. How should the participants be dressed?

43. ___________ meetings usually focus on arriving at a decision.
    a. problem-solving
    b. problem generating
    c. informational
    d. change facilitating
44. At a meeting, the __________ seating arrangement uses a round table so that status differences are minimized and all participants feel free to express their opinions.
    a. overly directive
    b. covertly directive
    c. participative
    d. combative
45. An agenda includes all of the following, except
    a. welcome
    b. apologies for absence
    c. apologies for rude behaviour
    d. minutes of the last meeting
46. The ____________ is generally a brief, accurate record of the business transacted at the previous meeting.
    a. notice
    b. agenda
    c. memoirs
    d. minutes
47. The minutes of meeting should be a precise and unambiguous
    a. precise and unambiguous
    b. written in the future tense
    c. personal and friendly
    d. rhetorical and sonorous
48. Which of these is not a suitable self-analysis question?
    a. What part time jobs have I held?
    b. Is my nose slightly crooked?
    c. Am I a leader?
    d. Have I done well in problem-solving courses?
49. 'Is the field I have chosen crowded, or is it short of workers?' This question is an example of a
    a. self-analysis question
    b. job-analysis question

c. career-analysis question
d. benefits-analysis question

50. Before you start structuring your resume, it would be a good idea to take ________of all the information you actually want to include.
a. glossary
b. directory
c. dormitory
d. inventory

51. The ________resume is organized around a series of skills and accomplishments, and employment and academic experience is put in subordinate sections.
a. biological
b. chronological
c. functional
d. etymological

52. A resume has all of the following sections, except
a. education
b. childhood experiences
c. work experience
d. special interests

53. Which of these entries in the work experience section of an applicant's resume is inappropriate?
a. June 1994—Auditor, Broke Investments
b. April 1996–December 1996—Volunteered for Red Cross
c. October 1996–March 1998—Staff Accountant Ruchi Foods
d. April 1998–June 2001—financial Analyst, Economic Times

54. To make your resume effective, you can do all of the following except
a. use facts, not opinions
b. present your strongest qualifications first
c. be as specific as possible about what you want to do
d. mention religious or political affiliations

55. _________resumes are scanned for input into a database
a. apathetic
b. traditional
c. electronic
d. electric

56. In the chronological resume, information about the applicant's educational qualifications and employment history is listed ________, in reverse order
    a. sequentially
    b. serendipitously
    c. seriously
    d. strategically
57. An application letter sent to a company in response to an advertisement of an opening is a ___________letter of application
    a. solvent
    b. solicited
    c. solicitous
    d. solemn
58. Which of these is not a characteristic of a well-written application letter?
    a. is of appropriate length
    b. is addressed to a person, not to a title
    c. reproduces the resume
    d. contains reader-benefit information
59. In an application letter statements like. 'This is an application', and 'Consider me an applicant for the post'. Are
    a. redundant
    b. redoubtable
    c. redolent
    d. refluent
60. To be effective, the opening of an application letter must not be
    a. specific
    b. written with care
    c. written from a 'you' viewpoint
    d. based on the 'I' attitude
61. Which of these would you say is an effective opening for a job application letter?
    a. Please consider me an applicant for the position that I recently learned was available in your company.
    b. I would like to have the opportunity to put my education and work experience to use as an employee in your company.

c. Your advertisement in The Economic Times, dated 21 October 2001, for an ambitious, hard-working sales representative, lists requirements similar to my qualifications. A degree in marketing and three years of sales experience make me confident of my ability to be the type of employee you would like to have in your company.
d. The article that I recently read about your company convinces me that your company would be an excellent place for me to begin my career. Please consider me for any opening in your company

62. In the middle section of the application letter you may include any of these except
    a. your understanding of the job requirements
    b. your understanding of the political climax in the country
    c. your educational achievements that qualify you for the job
    d. your work experience that helps qualify you for the position
63. As the application letter is ideally limited to one page, focus on your__________—something that the reader can use to his advantage.
    a. key bargaining point
    b. key selling point
    c. mesmerizing point
    d. key validating point
64. While ______________your key qualifications make sure you present your education and work achievements in such a manner that their significance to the job in question is immediately apparent.
    a. analysing
    b. summarizing
    c. elucidating
    d. flaunting
65. In an application letter, you can do all of the following except
    a. adopt a business-like tone
    b. boast about your abilities
    c. demonstrate your knowledge of the organization
    d. refer the reader to the enclosed resume
66. Which of these sentences is incorrect?
    (i) To function properly, the machine must be oiled every hour.
    (ii) If the machine is to function properly, you must oil it every hour

(iii) To function properly, you must oil the machine every hour.

a. 1
b. 2
c. 3
d. None of the above

67. A __________ is a direct statement of an idea that almost anyone would know already

a. precis
b. platitude
c. paragraph
d. preface

68. Pick the incorrect sentence

(i) Come to the office this a.m.
(ii) Come to the office at 10:15 a.m.
(iii) Come to the office this morning.

a. 1
b. 2
c. 3
d. None of the above

69. Which of these is a correct sentence?

(i) We were delighted at him taking the job.
(ii) We were delighted at his taking the job.
(iii) We were delighted at he taking the job.

a. 1
b. 2
c. 3
d. None of the above

70. I do not eat anything other than rice. Which of the four sentences given below have the same meaning as this sentence?

a. I only eat rice.
b. I eat only rice.
c. Only I eat rice.
d. Rice only I eat.

71. Limiting modifiers like________, ________, ______, ______, etc. must be carefully placed in order to convey the correct message.

a. why, what, how, where
b. only, almost, never, rarely

c. run, walk, talk, sleep.

d. he, she, it, they

72. ________sentences focus attention on the doer, and are therefore more vivid.

a. reactive

b. active

c. passive

d. assertive

73. Writers use _______ to help readers extract meaning from a sentence, in much the same way that speakers use pauses and voice inflexion.

a. abbreviations

b. alphabets

c. punctuation marks

d. italics

74. Pick the correct sentence

a. When I reached his house, the door was locked.

b. When I reached his house the door was locked.

c. When, I reached his house, the door, was locked.

d. When I reached his house, the door was locked.

75. Anjan watched __________as the rescue workers removed the charred remains of his furniture.

a. Sorrowing

b. Sorrowfully

c. Sorrow

d. Sorry

76. In which of these cases is a comma not used?

a. between coordinate clauses joined by but, for

b. between hours and minutes to express them in figures

c. after dependent clauses

d. between words in a series

77. Pick the correct sentence.

a. Mr. Mittal who is an engineer will move into the house.

b. Mr. Mittal who, is an engineer, will move into the house.

c. Mr. Mittal, who is an engineer, will move into the house.

d. Mr. Mittal who, is an engineer will, move into the house.

78. The sentence that expresses the central idea of a paragraph and draws together all the other sentences is called the
    a. major sentence
    b. thematic sentence
    c. topic sentence
    d. minor sentence
79. To achieve a logical progression of ideas and to provide coherence, writers use ________or 'transition' words.
    a. synthesizers
    b. illogical connectors
    c. logical connectors
    d. parentheses
80. The __________ like the topic sentence of a paragraph, expresses the author's main idea, around which the entire essay is built up.
    a. opening sentence
    b. rhetorical statement
    c. thesis statement
    d. storyline
81. Which of these should the introduction to the essay not do?
    a. capture the reader's attention
    b. present the concluding statement
    c. present the thesis statement
    d. give the reader an idea of what will follow
82. In an essay, the ______ from one idea to the next must not be abrupt.
    a. transportation
    b. transition
    c. transubstantiation
    d. transcription
83. ________ can help you to organize your ideas for writing an essay.
    a. An outline
    b. An introduction
    c. A preface
    d. A foreword
84. Sometimes the thesis statement in an essay is not openly stated, only ___________
    a. imploded
    b. implicated

c. implied
d. imbibed

85. In expressions that indicate ownership __________ indicates that a preposition has been left out.
a. a comma
b. a question mark
c. an asterisk
d. an apostrophe

86. Communication is made up of a chain of events that can be broken down into five phases.
a. sender, message, channel, receiver, feedback
b. seeker, message, channel, receiver, feedback
c. sender, letter, channel, receiver, feedback
d. sender, message, network, receiver, feedback

87. The sender is sometimes known as the
a. recorder
b. encoder
c. decider
d. beginner

88. In the internal communication network, a message flows in a
a. downward, upward, lateral or informal manner
b. distorted, upward, lateral or informal manner
c. downward, lateral, horizontal or informal manner
d. downward, upward, lateral or formal manner

89. Informal communication channels are often collectively referred to as
a. divine
b. vine
c. revive
d. grapevine

90. Successful managers tap into the informal communication channel by practising
a. ABA
b. AIDA
c. MBWA
d. BNL

91. Feedback is the receiver's response to the message some of the most common responses are designed to
    a. obtain more information or to provide closure
    b. retain more information or to provide closure
    c. to close the argument
    d. to bring the receiver closer to the speaker
92. Communication barriers can be placed in four categories
    a. problems caused by the sender, problems in message transmission, problems in reception, problems in receiver comprehension
    b. problems caused by the receiver, problems in message transmission, problems in reception, problems in sender comprehension
    c. problems caused by the sender static in the line, problems of message transmission, problems in reception, problems in receiver comprehension
    d. none of the above
93. To overcome communication barriers, it is essential to
    (i) know your subject
    (ii) focus on the purpose
    (iii) know your audience
        a. 2 and 3
        b. 1 and 2
        c. 1 and 3
        d. 2 and 3
94. Each communication situation is
    a. unusual
    b. unique
    c. ubiquitous
    d. none of the above
95. The three general speech purposes are
    (i) to inform
    (ii) to persuade
    (iii) to entertain
    (iv) to please
        a. 1 and 2
        b. 1, 2 and 3
        c. 2, 3 and 4
        d. None of the above

96. The purpose of informative communication is to
    (i) increase the receiver's knowledge and understanding of the subject
    (ii) increase the speaker's knowledge of the subject
    (iii) to run down the opposing speaker
        a. 2 and 3
        b. 2 only
        c. 1 and 2
        d. 1 only
97. 'Final examinations in our college should be abolished' This topic should be presented
    a. in a persuasive manner
    b. in a hilarious manner
    c. in a defiant manner
    d. none of the above
98. Which one of the following topics lends itself to humorous treatment?
    a. The gourmet food served in the college mess
    b. The history of air travel
    c. Nuclear bomb
    d. None of the above
99. A good specific speech purpose should
    (i) contain only one central idea
    (ii) be clear and concise
    (iii) be worded in terms of the desired audience response
        d. 1 and 2
        e. 1, 2 and 3
        f. 2 and 3
        g. none of the above
100. Which method of speech delivery puts no strain on your memory?
    a. speaking from a manuscript
    b. speaking from memory
    c. extemporaneous speaking
    d. none of the above
101. The extemporaneous delivery is often referred to as
    a. the last course
    b. the in-between course

c. the middle course
d. all of the above

102. When delivering your speech extemporaneously, notes should be written on
a. note pad
b. A-4 paper
c. small stiff cards
d. any of the above

103. Audience analysis enables you to establish a _________ with your listeners.
a. rapport
b. rash
c. reputation
d. none of the above

104. For a speech to be effective, the verbal and nonverbal elements of the presentation have to be
a. aligned
b. non-aligned
c. realigned
d. inclined

105. The body of a speech to inform can be organized in a
a. spatial pattern
b. causal pattern
c. topical pattern
d. any of the above

106. The 'body' of a speech to inform to can be organized in a variety of different ways, except
a. complex to simple
b. simple to complex
c. earliest to latest
d. none of the above

107. An introduction can gain the audience's attention through
a. a humorous quotation
b. an interesting narrative
c. a reference to a recent event
d. all of the above

108. A conclusion can be made even more memorable by the use of
   (i) a quotation
   (ii) an interesting illustration
   (iii) a challenge to the audience
      a. 1 and 2
      b. 2 and 3
      c. 1 and 3
      d. 1, 2 and 3

109. The problem-solution speech pattern is often used for
   a. persuasive speeches
   b. entertaining speeches
   c. informative speeches
   d. all of the above

110. The motivated sequence speech pattern consists of all these steps, except
   a. attention
   b. attraction
   c. need
   d. satisfaction

111. In the deductive speech structure,
   a. the proposal is not stated at all
   b. the proposal is stated last
   c. the proposal is stated first
   d. none of the above

112. In the inductive speech pattern,
   (i) the arguments are presented first
   (ii) the proposition is led up to
   (iii) there is no thesis
      a. 1 and 2
      b. 2 and 3
      c. 1 and 3
      d. 1, 2 and 3

113. Simple stating a point does not necessarily make a believable; assertions must be backed by proof. Which of the following does not help support an assertion?
   a. expert testimony
   b. illumination

c. statistics
d. none of the above

114. Handouts are a useful visual aid, but they can be distracting because
   a. people tend to read the material instead of listening to the presentation
   b. paper makes a lot of distracting noise
   c. the speaker forgets his lines because of the presence of handouts
   d. none of the above

115. Which of the following is not a visual aid/
   a. chalkboard
   b. slides
   c. analogies
   d. physical objects

116. Questions are often asked after an oral presentation. If you do not know the answer
   (i) make up an answer
   (ii) admit you do not know the answer
   (iii) suggest a possible way to obtain the answer
      a. 1
      b. 2
      c. 1 and 2
      d. 2 and 3

117. A letter written to persuade the reader to purchase a product
   (i) must focus on a central selling feature
   (ii) must have a 'you' attitude
   (iii) must be writer-centred
      a. 1, 2 and 3
      b. 1 and 3
      c. 2 and 3
      d. 1 and 2

118. When discussing price in an unsolicited sales letter
   (i) place the price discussion in the first paragraph
   (ii) state price in terms of small units
   (iii) mention price in a complex or compound sentence
      a. 1 and 2
      b. 1 and 3

c. 2 and 3
d. 1, 2 and 3

119. When writing a persuasive sales letter, our chances of getting the desired action from the readers is increased if we
(i) state the specific action wanted
(ii) present the action as being easy to take
(iii) show doubt about the reader's level of interest
a. 1
b. 2
c. 3
d. 1 and 2

120. Which of the following characteristics is not found in an effective collection series?
a. timeliness
b. regularity
c. aggression
d. stringency

121. Which of the following appeals is not used in a cover letter?
a. fair play
b. closure
c. pride
d. humour

122. In a collection letter, writers should use
a. one appeal
b. two appeals
c. three appeals
d. as many appeals as possible

123. The objective of a request memo is to gain a ________ response to a request
a. prompt
b. favourable
c. unfavourable
d. harsh

124. A confirmation memo is designed to _________ in writing something that has been agreed to verbally
a. confirm

b. confuse
c. firm
d. reaffirm

125. Periodic report memos are submitted at ______intervals
e. regulated
f. regular
g. irregular
h. meaningful

126. Memos that convey bad news need to be written
(i) inductively
(ii) with a positive tone
(iii) ambiguously
d. 1 and 2
e. 1
f. 1 and 3
g. 2 and 3

127. Which of the following is not included in a letter of transmittal?
a. Request for the report
b. Abstract
c. List of illustrations
d. Executive summary

128. Which of the following is not included in a letter of transmittal?
a. a statement of the title
b. an acknowledgement of any assistance received in preparing the material
c. a diagram showing the progress of the report
d. a statement of the principal results, conclusions and recommendations

129. The two basic types of abstracts are generally called
a. informative and informational abstracts
b. descriptive and executive abstracts
c. informative and executive abstracts
d. descriptive and informative abstracts.

130. In a report, the glossary is an alphabetical list of
a. definitions
b. symptoms

c. graphs
d. glossy pictures

131. In which part of the report would definitions of terms like CRT and SONAR be placed?
a. glossary
b. list of symbols
c. contents page
d. executive summary

132. Which of the following is generally not included in the introduction of the report?
a. a statement of the problem/purpose
b. a statement of the scope of the report
c. an analysis of the result
d. the background of the report

133. The conclusion of the report contains
(v) the key findings of the report
(vi) the writer's analysis of what the findings mean
(vii) opinions about the course of action that should be taken
a. 2
b. 1
c. 1 and 3
d. 1, 2 and 3

134. In informational reports, subtopics can be arranged in a variety of ways except
a. sequence
b. chronology
c. spatial orientation
d. imagination

135. Analytical reports generally follow a problem-solving method which problem-solving method is not followed?
a. hypothesis
b. relative merit
c. relative demerit
d. none of the above

136. Visual aids should be used in reports when they
(i) reinforce the material
(ii) simplify the material

(iii) clarify the material

a. 1 and 2
b. 2 and 3
c. 1 and 3
d. 1, 2 and 3

137. Illustrative material in a report only __________ the text, does not replace it.

a. supplements
b. positions
c. suspends
d. superscribes

138. In a visual aid, one should use

a. lots of attractive colours
b. numerous symbols
c. five different typefaces
d. none of the above

139. A visual aid in a report should ________ the reader.

(i) assist
(ii) subsist
(iii) alter

a. 1
b. 1 and 2
c. 2 and 3
d. 3

140. The writer should select the visual aid that best conveys his message. When presenting detailed _________ information, the writer should use a table, a systematic arrangement of data in columns and rows.

a. numerical
b. numbing
c. numerous
d. nullifying

141. An organization chart illustrates the

a. positions of an organization
b. units of an organization
c. functions of an organization
d. all of the above

142. In a report, a visual aid must be
   (i) in traduced in the text
   (ii) integrated into the text
   (iii) inverted in the text
      a. 1 only
      b. 3 only
      c. 1 and 2
      d. 2 and 3

143. A bad news letter written in a deductive style might __________ the reader
   (i) upset
   (ii) please
   (iii) annoy
      a. 1, 2 and 3
      b. 2 only
      c. 2 and 3
      d. 1 and 3

144. A good news or routine letter written in an inductive style might __________ the reader.
   (i) bore
   (ii) annoy
   (iii) terrify
      a. 1 and 2
      b. 2 only
      c. 1 and 2
      d. 3 only

145. If a bad news letter begins with a refusal and then follows it up with an explanation for the refusal
   a. the reader will most likely read the explanation
   b. the reader will accept the explanation with an open mind
   c. the reader will most likely not read the explanation with an open mind
   d. none of the above

146. In the communication process, the receiver of the message is also called the
   (i) decoder
   (ii) encoder

(iii) recorder

a. 3 only
b. 3 only
c. 1 and 3
d. 1 only

147. Your speech topic is 'The Indian Government should condemn American air raids on Iraq'. What kind of speech should you make?
a. predominantly informative
b. predominantly persuasive
c. predominantly entertaining
d. none of the above

148. Extemporaneous speaking calls for the speech to be
(i) researched
(ii) outlined
(iii) practised
(iv) delivered in a conversational manner

a. 1, 2, 3 and 4
b. 2 and 3
c. 1, 2 and 3
d. 3 and 4

149. What does a 'you'-attitude imply?
a. Think and write from your point of view.
b. Think and write from the reader's point of view.
c. Think and write from your mother's point of view.
d. None of the above

150. A letter informing a customer that the order cannot be filled and that the product requested will be substituted with another has to be worded very carefully. Above all, the word_______ should never be used.
a. superior
b. satisfaction
c. substitute
d. none of the above

151. What type of reports travel within an organization?
a. internal reports
b. external reports
c. annual reports
d. letter reports

152. When a report's purpose is to discover causes, predict results or suggest a solution to a problem, one way to proceed is to formulate__________ explanations.
   (i) hypothetical
   (ii) unbelievable
   (iii) problem-solving
      a. 1 and 2
      b. 2 and 3
      c. 1, 2 and 3
      d. 1 only

153. Communications scholars use the term________to refer to factors that interfere with the exchange of messages:
   a. deafness
   b. illness
   c. noise
   d. none of the above

154. Sounds that distract communicators fall into the category of
   a. physical noise
   b. psychological noise
   c. physiological noise
   d. none of the above

155. Hearing disorders interfere with the communication process. In what category can you put this type of interference?
   a. physiological noise
   b. physical noise
   c. psychological noise
   d. all of the above

156. What is wrong with this sales pitch? 'Gardeners are turning cartwheels in their excitement over our new weed killer'.
   (i) unbelievable
   (ii) lacking concrete proof
   (iii) not attention-getting
      a. 1 only
      b. 1 and 2
      c. 2 only
      d. 2 and 3

157. Solicited sales letters have been ________ by the prospect
   (i) invited
   (ii) rejected
   (iii) instigated
      a. 1 only
      b. 1 and 2
      c. 3 only
      d. 2 and 3
158. The term 'expert testimony' refers to the testimony of an
   (i) authority
   (ii) author
   (iii) undertaker
      a. 1, 2 and 3
      b. 2 only
      c. 3 only
      d. 1 only
159. Flip charts are effective in small, _____ groups.
   (i) informal
   (ii) formal
   (iii) executive
      a. 1 and 2
      b. 1 only
      c. 2 only
      d. 2 and 3
160. When numbering figures and tables in a report it is advisable to use
   (i) a single numbering system
   (ii) a dual numbering system
   (iii) no numbering
      a. 1 only
      b. 1 and 2
      c. 1 and 3
      d. 2 and 3
161. Any personal information that a respondent provides during an interview must be kept
   a. conventional
   b. confidential

c. conditional

d. convertible

162. The ________listener tunes in to the speaker's total message, both verbal and nonverbal.

a. selective

b. based

c. protective

d. active

163. Before writing a report the writer must ________ of his investigation by defining the problem.

a. conclude the process

b. narrow the focus

c. broaden the scope

d. appreciate the importance

164. If I ________I would exchange that typewriter for a personal computer

a. was her

b. were her

c. were she

d. was she

165. Each of our assistants________ required to take a short intensive training course.

a. are

b. were

c. is

d. none of the above

166. One of the major issues was ________ the concrete should be reinforced with steel.

a. whether or not

b. whether

c. why not

d. why ever not

167. In a speech to students, the ________ physical announced that the experiment had been successful

a. imminent

b. eminent

c. illuminated

d. framed

168. ________ the company has lost its first place position this year, next year's predictions are really promising.
    a. Although
    b. While
    c. Sometimes
    d. Notwithstanding

169. Although Rajan's request for promotion had been denied three times, his _____ was high.
    a. moral
    b. morale
    c. morality
    d. mortality

170. Two-thirds of the members think the _______ should be revised because of its ambiguity.
    a. statue
    b. stature
    c. statute
    d. status

171. The committee has been asked to prepare a practical ______ plan.
    a. equable
    b. equivocal
    c. eponymous
    d. equitable

172. Pick the correct sentence/s
    (i) Driving north, the vegetation became increasingly sparse.
    (ii) Driving north, we noticed that the vegetation became increasingly sparse.
    (iii) As we drove north, the vegetation became increasingly sparse
        a. 1 only
        b. 1 and 3
        c. 2 and 3
        d. 3 only

173. Pick the correct sentence/s
    (i) When in diapers, my mother remarried.
    (ii) When I was in diapers, my mother remarried.
    (iii) When in diapers, I attended my mother's second wedding.

a. 1 only
b. 1 and 3
c. 2 and 3
d. 3 only

174. Pick the correct sentence/s
   (i) to express themselves, graffiti decorate walls.
   (ii) graffiti decorate walls to express themselves.
   (iii) to express themselves, some youths decorate walls with graffiti.
   a. 1 only
   b. 1 and 3 only
   c. 1 and 2 only
   d. 2 and 3 only

16

Vocabulary

I. APPROPRIATE PREPOSITIONS

Prepositions must suit not only the sense intended by the writer, but also the idiom imposed by custom. A particular preposition stands in a particular phrase or context, for

1. **Abide with** (a person). 'I will *abide with* you in all circumstances'.
   Abide by (a thing). 'He did not *abide by* my decision'.
   Abide at (a place). 'I shall *abide at* the station before you come'.
   Abide in (a house). 'These days I am *abiding in* my friend's house'.
2. **Accused of** (a crime). 'He was *accused of* theft'.
   Accused by (a person). 'He was *accused by* his brother'.
3. **Apply for** (a thing). 'He *applied for* the post of lecturer'.
   Apply to (a person). 'He *applied to* the Principal'.
4. **Appeal to** (a person). 'They *appealed to* the judge'.
   Appeal against (a thing). 'They *appealed against* the decision of the magistrate'.
5. **Angry at** (a thing). 'I am *angry at* your behaviour'.
   Angry for (refers to action). 'I am *angry for* your disobeying me'.
   Angry with (a place). 'I am *angry with* you'.
6. **Arrive in** (a person). 'He *arrived at* Agra'.
   Arrive at (a country). 'He *arrived in* India'.
7. **Admit of** (a thing). 'What you have done *admits of* excuse.'
   Admit to or **into** (a place). 'He was *admitted to* the school'.
8. **Alight on** (the ground, a thing). 'The birds *alight on* the roof of a temple'.
   Alight at (a place). 'He *alighted* from his horse *at* my gate.'
   Alight from (a horse or carriage). 'At last he *alighted from* his horse'.

9. **Amuse at** (a thing). 'I was greatly *amused at* his ignorance'.
   Amuse with (refers to action). 'The children *amused* themselves *with* throwing stones at the frogs'.
10. **Annoyed at** (a thing). 'He was *annoyed at* my absence'.
    Annoyed with (a person). 'He was *annoyed* with me'.
11. **Answer to** (a thing). 'How will you *answer to* him?'
    Answer for (a thing). 'How will you *answer for* your conduct?'
12. **Antipathy to** (a thing). 'I have a great *antipathy to* meet'.
    Antipathy against (a person). 'We should not have any *antipathy against* others'.
13. **Anxious about** (the result of something). 'I am very *anxious about* his success in the examination'.
    Anxious for (safely, health). 'I am very *anxious for* his safety'.
14. **Ask from** (a person). 'I *asked* some money *from* him'.
    Ask for (a thing). 'I *asked* him *for* some money'.
15. **Affiliated to** (a university or board). 'In the beginning, Agra College was *affiliated to* the University of Calcutta'.
    Affiliated with (a part). 'Socialists were *affiliated with* the Congress party'.
16. **Arm** oneself **against** (a danger). 'We should *arm* ourselves in time *against* danger'.
    Arm oneself **with** (weapons). 'He *armed* himself *with* a sword and a rifle'.
17. **Atone to** (a person). 'He tried to *atone to* me by offering a sum of money'.
    Atone for (a thing). 'He tried to *atone for* the injury he had done'.
18. **Attend to** (a thing). 'I did not *attend to* what he said'.
    Attend upon (serve a person). 'He has no servant to *attend upon* him'.
19. **Award for** (a thing). 'Three prizes were *awarded for* proficiency in Mathematics'.
    Award to (a person). 'I want to *award* a silver cup *to* the best boy of my college'.
20. **Account for** (a thing). '*Account for* your absence from the hostel'.
    Account to (a person). 'He will *account for* his fault *to* the Principal'.
21. **Argue against or about** (a thing). 'I *argue against* the Hindu Code Bill'.
    Argue with (a person). 'Do not *argue with* me'.

22. **Apologize for** (a thing). 'I must *apologize for* not replying to your letter'.
Apologize to (a person). 'I must *apologize to* you'.

22a. **Appoint** (a person). 'I *appointed* him a lecturer'.
Appoint to (a situation). 'I *appointed* him *to* the post of a lecturer'.

23. **Arbitrate between** (two parties.) 'He was asked to *arbitrate between* them'.
Arbitrate in (a dispute). 'He was asked to *arbitrate in* a dispute about the short delivery of goods'.

24. **Accomplice with** (a person). 'This fellow was an *accomplice with* the thief'.
Accomplice in (some crime). 'This fellow was an *accomplice in* house-breaking'.

25. **Affinity with** (something). 'The short story has great *affinity with* the novel'.
Affinity between (two things). 'There is a great *affinity between* the novel and the short story'.

26. **Antidote to** (medicine for position). 'Diamond is regarded as an *antidote to* the position of the snake.'
Antidote against (infection). 'Quinine is an *antidote against* malaria'.

27. **Authority over** (a person). 'I have no *authority over* him in this matter'.
Authority on (a subject). 'He is a great *authority on* Ancient Indian History'.
Authority for (refers to action). 'He has no *authority for* abusing me'.

28. **Aspire to** (a situation). 'He *aspires to* the post of the Principal'.
Aspire after (fame). 'Those who *aspire after* cheap popularity can never serve the society'.

29. **Agree with** (a person). 'I do not *agree with* him'.
Agree to (a proposal). 'He *agreed to* all the proposals we made'.
Agree on (an option). 'I *agree* with you *in* opinion you have expressed'.
Agree on (a subject). 'After much discussion, they *agreed on* the terms of partnership'.

30. **Accommodate** oneself **to** (circumstance). 'We must *accommodate* ourselves *to* our circumstances'.
Accommodate a person **with** (lodging or loan). 'I *accommodated* my friend *with* lodgings'.

31. **Ambitious for** (a thing). 'We should not be *ambitious for* wealth'.
Ambitious of (fame). 'I am not *ambitious of* such a distinction'.

32. **Beg of** or **from** (a person). 'I *begged of* him to give me some money'. 'I *begged* some money *from* him'.
Beg a person **for** (a thing). 'I *begged* him *for* some money'.

33. **Beloved by** (verb). 'He is greatly *beloved by* his father'.
Beloved of (noun). 'She is a *beloved of* my friend'.

34. **Blind in** (one eye). 'He is *blind in* the left eye'.
Blind to (one's own defects). 'He is *blind to* his misdeeds'.

35. **Born in** (a country). 'He was *born in* England'.
Born of (parents). 'He was *born of* an intelligent stock'.

36. **Busy at** (a thing). 'I am *busy* at work'.
Busy with (refer to action). 'I am *busy with* work'.

37. **Buy** a thing **from** (a shop). 'You cannot *buy* this medicine at control rate *from* any shop'.
Buy a thing **of** (a person). 'I *bought* this medicine *of* my friend'.

38. **Cause for** (anxiety). 'You do not have any *cause for* anxiety'.
Cause of (trouble). 'He is the chief *cause of* all the nuisance'.

39. **Claim on** (a person). 'I have a *claim on* him'.
Claim to (a thing). 'I have a *claim to* his property'.

40. **Compete with** (a person). 'He will *compete with* me'.
Compete for (a thing). 'He will *compete for* the prize'.

41. **Conformity with** (views etc.). 'I acted in *conformity with* the advice of my father'.
Conformity to (a rule). 'I did that in *conformity to* the ancient custom'.

42. **Contribute to** (a fund). 'He *contributed* Rs. 500/– to our Children's Welfare Association'.

43. **Contribution towards** (some project). 'The *contribution* of Prem Chand *towards* the development of Hindi fiction is considerable'.

44. **Controversy with** (a person). 'I do not have any *controversy with* him'.
Controversy on or **about** (a thing). 'There was a good deal of *controversy on* the question of passing the Hindu Code Bill'.

45. **Condole with** (a person). 'I *condoled with* him'.
Condole in (a mishap). 'I *condoled in* his father's death'.

46. **Complain against** (a person). 'I have to *complain against* him for his rude behaviour'.
Complain of (a thing). 'I have to *complain of* his rude behaviour'.

47. **Consult with** (a person). 'You should *consult with* some expert doctor'.
Consult on (a thing). 'We *consulted on* the new programme'.

48. **Compare with** (show points of resemblance as well as of difference between two things of the same class). 'Kalidas is *compared with* Shakespeare'.
Compare to (show points of resemblance only between two things of the different classes). 'Anger is *compare to* fire'.

49. **Close to** (adjective). 'His house is quite *close to* mine'.
Close with (verb). 'I at once *closed with* his talks'.

50. **Clothed in** (dress). 'He was *clothed in* silk'.
Clothed with (some quality). 'He was *clothed with* shame'.

51. **Confide in** (a person). 'I *confide in* him and he has never deceived me'.
Confide a thing to (a person). 'Do not *confide* your secrets to everyone'.

52. **Care about** (a thing). 'I do not *care about* his health'.

53. **Charge against** (a person). 'He brought a *charge against* me'.
Charge a person with (a crime). 'He *charged* me with theft'.

54. **Condemn to** (a certain punishment). 'He was *condemned to* death'.
Condemn for (a certain crime). 'He was *condemned for* robbery'.

55. **Confer with** (consult with a person). She *conferred with* her husband'.
Confer about (consult about a thing). 'They *conferred* together *about* opening a new college'.

55a. **Consist in** (means remain). 'The beauty of this poem *consists in* its style'.
Consist of (means composed of). 'The body *consists of* bones, flesh, etc.'

56. **Converse with** (a person). 'I *converse* with him'.
Converse on or about (a thing). 'I *conversed* with him *on* various topics'.

57. **Correspond with** (a person). 'I *corresponded with* him two years ago'.
Correspond about (a thing). 'I *corresponded about* his business prospects'.

58. **Commence on** (a day). 'Examinations will *commence on* Monday next'.
Commence with (a book). 'He *commenced with* History'.

59. **Concerned at or about** (affected by). 'I am quite *concerned about* my father's illness'.
Concerned in (interested in). 'These two men were *concerned in* the business'.
Concerned for (anxious for). 'I am greatly *concerned for* the safety of his money'.

60. **Convenient for** (means suitable). 'This house is *convenient* for me'.
Convenient to (means easy). 'It is not now *convenient to* me to write a letter'.

61. **Clash against** (means to strike against). 'The swords *clashed against* their armour'.
Clash with (means to come in conflict with). 'His interests *clash with* my own'.

62. **Capable of** (a thing). 'He is not *capable of* such means acts'.
Capacity for (doing thing). 'He has a great *capacity for* mastering facts and dates'.

63. **Connect to** (means to join, combine). 'We *connect* one word *to* another to make a compound'.
Connect with (means to establish connection, relationship). 'We *connect* natural events *with* moral causes'.

64. **Dwell among** (people). 'He was *dwelling among* strangers'.
Dwell at (a place). 'These days I am *dwelling at* my friend's house'.
Dwell in (a country). 'The Aryas *dwelt in* Asia Minor'.
Dwell on or upon (a subject). 'The speaker *dwelt upon* the importance of hard work'.

65. **Disgusted at** (a thing). 'I am *disgusted at* your behaviour'.
Disgusted with (a person or life). 'I am *disgusted with* college life'.

66. **Displeased with** (a person). 'He is greatly *displeased with* me'.
Displeased at (a thing). 'I am never *displeased at* the fun of children'.

67. **Disqualified for** (a post). 'He is *disqualified for* the election'.
Disqualified from (competing). 'He was *disqualified from* taking part in the election'.

68. **Destined for** (means to be created for). 'God has *destined* him *for* a higher position than he now holds'.
Destined to (means subject to). 'He is *destined to* endless suffering'.

69. **Dine on** (a thing). 'It is not pleasant to *dine* daily *on* the same kind of food'.
Dine with (a person). 'I will *dine with* him tonight'.

70. **Discontented at** (difficulties). 'We should not be *discontented at* ordinary troubles'.
Disconnected with (what we posses). 'He is utterly *discontented with* his salary'.

71. **Die of** (a disease). 'He *died of* consumption'.
Die from (some cause). 'He *died from* overwork'.

72. **Differ with** (a person. 'I *differ with* you as to the exact meaning of this word'.
Differ from (a thing). 'How does prose *differ from* poetry'?
Differ on (a point). 'Opinions *differ* sharply *on* this subject'.

73. **Disappointed in** (a person). ‘I am *disappointed in* him, for I thought him honest, but he has proved a rogue’.
Disappointed with (a thing). ‘I was *disappointed with* the book when I read it’.

74. **Deal by** (means to behave towards a person). ‘This gentleman *deals* well *by* his clerks’.
Deal in (means to trade in). ‘The merchant *deals in* silk goods’.
Deal out (means to distribute). ‘A judge should *deal out* equal justice to all’.
Deal with (means to have to do with a thing). ‘This book *deals with* questions of Political Economy’.

75. **Decide on** (a thing). ‘He has not *decided on* this matter yet’.
Decide for or against (a person). ‘The cause was *decided* against him’.

76. **Declare against** (the happening of a new thing). ‘The municipality has *declared against* building a new bridge’.
Declare for (a thing). ‘The fighting nations should now *declare for* peace’.

77. **Dispense with** (means to do without). ‘You can easily *dispense with* his services’.
Dispense to (means to deal out or distribute). ‘He *dispenses* equal justice *to* all’.

78. **Dispose of** (means to sell). ‘He has *disposed of* all his goods’.
Dispose to (means to incline a person to a thing). ‘The news of his father’s death *disposed* him *to* great sorrow’.

79. **Dispute about** (a thing). ‘The farmer *disputed about* the division of his land’.
Dispute with (a person). ‘I do not want to *dispute with* you on this point’.

80. **Enquire of** (a person). ‘I *enquired of* him the way to the station’.
Enquire into (a matter). ‘The Inspector is vigorously *enquiring into* the case of misappropriation’.

81. **Embark on** (a new business speculation). ‘I have *embarked on* a very risky enterprise’.
Embark on (a vessel). ‘He *embarked on* the ship for England’.

82. **Enter into** (an engagement, into conversation, into an alliance, into a contest, into a contract, into a discussion, into possession). ‘I *entered into* new agreement with him’.
Enter upon (a work, upon a course, upon a law–suit, upon a war). ‘He has *entered upon* a new course of life’.

83. **Exchange** a thing **with** (a person). 'Will you *exchange* pencils *with* me'.
Exchange for (a thing). 'I *exchanged* a book *for* a fountainpen'.

84. **Exult at** (success). 'It is natural for him to *exult at* his own success'.
Exult over (a defeated enemy). 'We should not *exult over* a fallen foe'.
Exult in (rejoice). 'Do not *exult in* the miseries of others'.

85. **Eager for** (fame, for praise). 'He is *eager for* making a name for himself'.
Eager in (a search). 'He threw himself *eagerly in* the pursuit of knowledge'.

86. **Enraged at** (a thing). 'I am *enraged at* his behaviour'.
Enraged with (a person). 'I am *enraged with* him for speaking against me'.

87. **Equal to** (means to be able to do). 'He is not *equal to* the task'.
Equal with (a person). 'He suffered *equally with* the rest'.

88. **Educated in** (something). 'He is *educated in* scientific subjects.'
Educated for (some profession). 'He is *educated for* technical works'.

89. **Enamoured with** (a person). 'He is *enamoured with* her'.
Enamoured of (a thing). 'He is *enamoured of* her charms'.

90. **Elated at** (success). 'He was greatly *elated at* his success'.
Elated with (joy). 'He was *elated with* joy'.

91. **Equivalent for** (a work). 'Give an *equivalent for* this word'.
Equivalent to (a sum of money). 'A shilling is *equivalent to* seventy-five paise'.

92. **Exact from** (a person; verb). 'Heavy fines were *exacted from* the villagers'.
Exact in (a thing; adjective). 'He is not *exact in* payment'.

93. **Expert in** (doing a thing). 'He is *expert in* deceiving others':
Expert at (a thing). 'He is *expert at* accounts'.

94. **Entrust a person with** (a thing). 'I *entrusted* his *with* hundred pounds'.
Entrust a thing **to** (a person). 'I *entrusted* a hundred pounds *to* him'.

95. **Fight against** (a country). 'We should not *fight against* our country'.
Fight for (the sake of defending the week against the strong). 'He *fought for* his country'.
Fight with or **against** (a person). 'In the last War Japan *fought with* Germans *against* the allies'.

96. **Furnish** a thing **to** (a person). 'We should *furnish* food *to* the hungry'.
Furnish a person **with** (a thing). 'I *furnished* the servant *with* money to buy food for me'.

97. **Familiar to** (things are familiar to persons). 'His face is quite *familiar to* me'.
Familiar with (persons are familiar with things). 'He is perfectly *familiar with* Hindu mythology'.

98. **Fascinated by** (a thing). 'I was *fascinated by* her looks'.
Fascinated with (a person). 'I was *fascinated with* her'.

99. **Feed on or upon** (means to live on). 'The cow *feeds on* grass'.
Feed with (some eatable). 'I *feed* the baby *with* milk'.

100. **False of** (heart). 'He is not *false of* heart'.
False to (friends or principles). 'We should not be *false to* our friends'.

101. **Guard against** (mistakes, temptations etc.). 'We should *guard against* grammatical errors'.
Guard from (a danger of a thief etc.). 'God will *guard* us *from* all dangers'.

102. **Good at** (something). 'This gentleman is *good at* cricket'.
Good for (nothing). 'He is *good for* nothing'.

103. **Grateful to** (a person). 'I feel very *grateful to* you'.
Grateful for (a thing). 'Always be *grateful for* kindness'.

104. **Glance at** (a sight). 'He *glanced at* the stranger's face'.
Glanced over (a writing). 'He *glanced over* the letter'.

105. **Grieve at** (an event). 'He *grieved at* my father's passing away'.
Grieve for (a person). 'He *grieved for* me'.
Grieve over (a thing). 'He is *grieved over* my loss'.

II. THE SAME WORD USED AS DIFFERENT PARTS OF SPEECH

The grammatical character of a word is determined by its use or function. We cannot say that particular word is a noun or a verb unless we study its position in the given sentence. The following are some of important words which may belong to different parts of speech, according to the way in which they are used. It is supposed that a careful study of this list will help the student increasing his grammatical knowledge of words.

1. **A—**
Indefinite Article. The sportsman shot *a* tiger.
Preposition. He has gone *a* hunting.

2. **All—**
Noun. He lost his *all* in gambling.
Adjective. *All* men are mortal.
Adverb. He is now *all* right.
Pronoun. *All* were in favour of going there.

3. **Any—**
   Pronoun. Does *any* of you know anything about it?
   Adjective. Take *any* book that you like most.
   Adverb. We must rest before going *any* further.

4. **As—**
   Pronoun. He is not such a fool *as* looks.
   Adverb. We walked *as* fast as we could.
   Conjunction. *As* he was poor I helped him.

5. **About—**
   Adverb. She wandered *about* in silken garments.
   Preposition. There is something pleasing *about* him.

6. **Above—**
   Noun. Our blessings come from *above*.
   Adverb. The heavens are *above*.
   Preposition. The moral law is *above* the civil.

7. **After—**
   Adjective. *After* ages she'd sing his glory.
   Adverb. They arrived soon *after*.
   Conjunction. We went away *after* they had left.
   Preposition. He looks *after* his father.

8. **Age—**
   Noun. In *age* he is younger than I.
   Verb. You are *aging*, my darling.

9. **Arm—**
   Noun. He received a deadly wound in his *arm*.
   Verb. They were asked to *arm* themselves with weapons.

10. **Before—**
    Adverb. I have not seen you *before*.
    Conjunction. He went away *before* I came.

11. **Better—**
    Noun. Give place to your *betters*.
    Adjective. I think yours is a *better* plan.
    Verb. Let us first *better* our economic position.
    Adverb. You are working *better* today.

12. **Both—**
    Pronoun. *Both* of them are gone.
    Adjective. You cannot have it *both* ways.
    Conjunction. *Both* the cashier and the accountant are on.

13. **Boil—**
Noun. He is suffering from a bad *boil.*
Verb. Boil the eggs, please.

14. **But—**
Pronoun. There is no one *but* likes him.
Adverb. It is *but* natural.
Conjunction. We tried hand, *but* did not succeed.
Preposition. None *but* the brave deserve the praise.

15. **Back—**
Noun. He carried the load on his *back.*
Verb. Do not *back* a wrong cause.

16. **Book—**
Noun. I am writing a *book* on grammar.
Verb. My luggage is *booked* for this train.

17. **Bare—**
Adjective. He has *bare* feet.
Adverb. He walked *bare* headed.
Verb. Bare your arm.

18. **By—**
Adverb. Time passes *by.*
Preposition. He was much loved *by* his mother.

19. **Close—**
Noun. The meeting came to a *close* at 4 p.m.
Adjective. They are very *close* friends.
Verb. The college will *close* tomorrow.
Adverb. They walked *close* to each other.

20. **Calm—**
Noun. 'The *calm* of mind, all position spent' is the effect of a tragedy.
Adjective. The atmosphere here is very *calm* and quiet.
Verb. First *calm* yourself and then do what you think desirable.

21. **Cold—**
Noun. Do not go out lest you should catch *cold.*
Adjective. It is very *cold* this evening.

22. **Court—**
Noun. He is summoned to the *court* of law.
Verb. Why do your *court* death unnecessarily?

23. **Cane—**
Noun. He has a beautiful *cane.*
Verb. He was *caned* publicly.

24. **Cut—**
    Noun. I do not like the *cut* of your moustaches.
    Verb. *Cut* your coat according to your cloth.

25. **Cover—**
    Noun. Use a *cover* over your book.
    Verb. It is very cold, *cover* your head.

26. **Down—**
    Noun. He has seen the ups and *downs* of life.
    Adjective. The porter was killed by the *down* train.
    Verb. *Down* with tyranny.
    Adverb. *Down* went all his hopes.
    Preposition. The fire engine came rushing *down* the hill.

27. **Deep—**
    Noun. He fell down into the *deep*.
    Adjective. It is a very *deep* well.
    Adverb. The cap fell *deep* into the tank.

28. **Drive—**
    Noun. My father has gone out for a *drive*.
    Verb. He was *driving* very fast.

29. **Date—**
    Noun. His *date* of birth is not known.
    Verb. The Bikrami era *dates* from 57 B.C.

30. **Either—**
    Pronoun. Ask *either* of them to bring water.
    Adjective. *Either* pen is good enough.
    Conjunction. He must *either* work or starve.

31. **Enough—**
    Adjective. There is time *enough* to spare.
    Adverb. You know well *enough* what I mean.

32. **Even—**
    Adjective. The chances are *even*.
    Verb. Let us *even* the ground.
    Adverb. You cannot *even* see him.

33. **Except—**
    Verb. If we *except* him, all are to be blamed.
    Conjunction. I will not let thee *except* (unless) thou bless you.
    Preposition. All the members of his family were there *except* his wife.

34. **Else—**
Adjective. I have something *else* for you.
Adverb. Shall we look anywhere *else*.
Conjunction. Make haste, *else* you should miss the train.

35. **Eye—**
Noun. He saw nature with the *eye* of a scientist as well.
Verb. The constable *eyed* the beggar with suspicion.

36. **Elder—**
Noun. We must show respect to our *elders*.
Adjective. He is my *elder* brother.

37. **For—**
Conjunction. We should help him *for* he is very poor.
Preposition. I was looking *for* you.

38. **Fast—**
Noun. Let us observe a *fast* today.
Adjective. He is a very *fast* runner.
Verb. He *fasted* for a week.
Adverb. He ran so *fast* that he tumbled down.

39. **Free—**
Adjective. India is now a *free* country.
Verb. Let us *free* ourselves from bondage.

40. **Fix—**
Noun. He was in a terrible *fix* then.
Verb. *Fix* some other time for our meeting.

41. **Fill—**
Noun. We ate to our *fill*.
Verb. *Fill* this pen with ink.

42. **Face—**
Noun. There are red pimples on his *face*.
Verb. He *faced* the situation boldly.

43. **Fool—**
Noun. He was a *fool* to act like that.
Verb. You cannot *fool* all people for all times.

44. **Fish—**
Noun. A whale is a kind of large *fish*.
Verb. Do not *fish* in troubled waters.

45. **Fell—**
Adjective. Tuberculosis is a *fell* disease.
Verb. He *fell* down from the roof of his house.

III. THE SAME WORD IN DIFFERENT PHRASES

Bear

1. **Bear down** (overthrow, or crush by force). 'They were *borne down* by the enemy's large force.'
2. **Bear down upon** (approach with a fair wind). 'The fleet *bore down upon* the enemy.'
3. **Bear out** (support or confirm). 'Your statement is not *borne out* by facts.'
4. **Bear through** (manage; to support to the end). 'Religion can *bear* man *through* all the ills of life.'
5. **Bear up** (support; keep from falling or striking; to be firm; not to sink). 'His patience alone *bore* him *up* in his troubles.' 'I must try to *bear up* against his misfortune.'
6. **Bear with** (endure; tolerate). 'A sincere man should *bear with* his friend's shortcomings.'
7. **Bear upon or on** (to be connected with). 'Your remarks do not *bear upon* the subject in hand.'

Beat

1. **Beat down** (destroy; crush; lesson). 'To *beat down* a wall; 'to *beat down* opposition'; 'to *beat down* the price of an article.'
2. **Beat off** (drive back). 'The enemy was *beaten off*.'
3. **Beat up** (gather; search out and collect). 'He went round to all his friends to *beat up* meeting.'

Blow

1. **Blow out** (extinguish). '*Blow out* all the lights.'
2. **Blow up** (explode). 'A matchstick is enough to *blow up* a petrol tank.'
3. **Blow upon** (taint; blast). 'I will not allow my reputation to *blow upon*.'
4. **Blow over** (pass away without injurious effect). 'The cloud of misfortune has now *blown over*.'

Break

1. **Break down** (1. come down by breaking. 2. fail in an undertaking. 3. to be overwhelmed). 'The coach *broke down* midway.' 'He *broke down* in the middle of his speech.' 'The poor boy was *broken down* with grief at his mother's death.'

2. **Break forth** (burst out). 'He *broke forth* into shouts of gladness.' 'Hearing this, the prisoner *broke forth* into loud appeals for mercy.'

Bring

1. **Bring about** (cause to happen). 'I do not know what has *brought about* this wonderful change in his character.'
2. **Bring back** (recall; remember). 'I could not *bring back* his name of memory.'
3. **Bring forth** (near; as offspring). 'The lioness *brings forth* only one cub in a year'.
4. **Bring in** (product; introduce). 'His property *brings in* Rs. 1,000 a year'. 'Strange fashions have recently been *brought in*.'
5. **Bring on** (cause to bring). 'Cold *brings on* fever.'
6. **Bring out** (show or expose). '*Bring out* the meaning of this paragraph.' 'The investigation is sure to *bring out* some surprising results.'
7. **Bring over** (draw to a new party). 'They soon *brought* him *over* to the side of the Government.' 'Three Hindus have recently been *brought over* to Mohammedanism.'
8. **Bring to** (restore to consciousness). 'He fainted, and was *brought to* sense with great difficulty.'
9. **Bring up** (1. educate 2. finish). 1. '*Bring up* a child in the habits of truth and honesty.' 2. 'The manager of the hotel will not give him anything on credit unless he *brings up* his arrears.'

Call

1. **Call at** (visit). 'When I *called at* his house, he gave me a warm reception.'
2. **Call to account** (demand an explanation from). 'He was *called to account* for his conduct in that affairs.'
3. **Call back** (revoke; summon back). 'I will not *call back* any of my statements.' 'The Governor was *called back* at once.'
4. **Call down** (invoke; bring down). 'They *call down* the anger of God upon their enemy.' 'He will *call down* thunderbolts from heaven.'
5. **Call forth** (bring into action). 'This work will *call forth* all his energies.' 'His remarks *called forth* much opposition.'
6. **Call for** (demand or require). 'This statement *calls for* no remark.' 'This offence *calls for* a great punishment.'

7. **Call in** (collect; withdraw from circulation). '*Call in* debts.' '*Call in* uncurrent coins.'
8. **Call off** (to summon away; to divert). 'He *called off* my attention.' 'I *called off* workmen from their employment.'
9. **Call names** (abuse). 'When I refused to accept this views, he began to *call* me *names*.'
10. **Call on or upon** (1. make a short visit to 2. invoke). 'I *called on* my friend before I left.' '*Call upon* me in the hour of trouble.'
11. **Call out** (speak aloud; call to service; challenge to fight). 'I *called out* to him from a distance.' 'He *called* his opponent *out*, but the fellow was too great a coward to come.'
12. **Call up** (bring to view or recollection). 'Can you *call up* the image of an absent friend?'

Carry

1. **Carry off** (1. kill; 2. bear away). 'When the epidemic broke out in the district, thousands of people were *carried off*.' 'The wind *carried off* the smell.'
2. **Carry on** (continue). 'He *carried on* his studies even after his failure.'
3. **Carry out** (accomplish; execute). 'I shall *carry out* your orders.'
4. **Carry through** (sustain or support to the end). 'His labour and honesty *carried* him *through* all difficulties.'

Cast

1. **Cash about for** (try to get). 'As son as the book was ready for publication, he began to *cast about* for subscribers.'
2. **Caste aside** (reject as useless). 'He soon got tired of his job and *cast it aside* for a new one.'
3. **Cast away** (throw away; reject). 'Such a golden opportunity should not be *cast away*'. 'We were *caste away* on a barren island.'
4. **Cast out** (throw or turn out). 'The man was charged of *casting out* evil spirits with the aid of the Devil.'
5. **Cast down** (dejected; depressed). 'He looks *cast down* after his recent loss.'
6. **Cast eyes on** (see). 'He is the ugliest man I have never *cast eyes on*.'
7. **Cast off** (reject or discard). 'His relatives and friends have *cast* him *off* entirely.'

8. **Cast up** (compute). 'You had better carefully *cast up* the expense of his elaborate scheme before you undertake it.'

Come

1. **Come about** (happen). 'How did this sad event *come about*.'
2. **Come by** (get). 'He *came by* his wealth by dishonest means.'
3. **Come in** (be brought into use or fashion). 'The custom *came in* with the British rule.'
4. **Come of** (issue from; to be borne in). 'Shri J.L. Nehru *came of* a rich and respectable family.'
5. **Come off** (1. emerge; come out, 2. take place). 'He *came off* successful at the B.A. examination.' 2. 'When does Dussehra festival *come off?*'
6. **Come on** (approach). 'Winter is *coming on*.'
7. **Come out** (become public). 'The matter has *come out* at last.'
8. **Come to one's self** (recover consciousness). 'He fainted and it was a long while before he *came to himself*.'
9. **Come upon** (1. fall upon; attack, 2. meet with). 1. 'They *come upon* the enemy all of a sudden.' 2. On their way the accidentally *came upon* an obstacle and had to turn back.'
10. **Come up** (amount to). 'His debts *come up* to a thousand rupees.'

Cry

1. **Cry down** (condemn). 'We should not *cry down* a book simply because we dislike the author.'
2. **Cry up** (praise). 'A merchant will naturally *cry up* his goods.'
3. **Cry out** (scream; complain loudly). 'Do not *cry out* before you are hurt.'

Do

1. **Do away with** (put an end). 'The custom has been *done away with*.'
2. **Do by** (treat). 'Do as you would be *done by*.'
3. **Do for** (answer or be sufficient for). 'This will *do for* my purpose.'
4. **Do up** (pack up). 'My pillow is *done up* in the bundle'.
5. **Have done with** (have no further concern with). 'I *have done with* him.'
6. **Do without** (dispense with). 'We should learn to *do without luxuries*.'
7. **Do with** (dispose of; employ). 'What am I to *do with* this money.'

Draw

1. **Draw back** (retire). 'I will not *draw back* whatever the difficulties in my way may be.'
2. **Draw off** (retire). 'He *drew off* his forces form the field.'
3. **Draw on or upon** (obtain money from, by a draft or order). 'I have *drawn on* the bank for a large sum of money.'
4. **Draw out** [outlead, detach, or array (troops), prolong, elicit, induce to talk; write out in proper form; (of days) become longer]. The opposition put many ticklish questions in order to *draw* the minister *out*. He *drew out* his remarks to a great length. He *draws out* his sword to kill him.
5. **Draw up** (compose). 'He has been asked to *draw up* the petition.'

Fall

1. **Fall away** (1. lose flesh 2. decrease in number). 1. 'He has *fallen away* a great deal since his illness.' 2. 'His followers *fell away* rapidly.'
2. **Fall from** (withdraw from). 'He has *fallen from* agreement.'
3. **Fall in with** (1. agree with 2. meet with). 1. 'He *fell in with* my views.' 2. 'On the way he *fell in with* thieves.'
4. **Fall off** (1. withdraw or become separated, 2. perish; die away, 3. drop). 1. 'Friends *fall off* in bad days.' 2. 'Words *fall off* by disuse.' 3. 'Fruits *fell down* when ripe.'
5. **Fall on** (attack). 'They *fell on* him and threw him down.'
6. **Fall out** (1. quarrel. 2. happen or befall). 1. 'The dogs *fell out* over a bone and attacked each other fiercely.' 2. 'It so *fell out* that no guard was on duty that night.'
7. **Fall short of** (to be less than). 'The result *fell short of* expectations.'
8. **Fall under** (1. come under. 2. be placed in). 'These things do not *fall under* human sight or observation.' 2. 'These substances *fall under* a different classes.'
9. **Fall back** (retreat; get back). 'The rebels *fell back* to a place of safety.'
10. **Fall through** (come to nothing). 'As nobody supported him, his resolution *fell through*.' 'The scheme you made for building a new house has *fallen through* for lack of funds.'
11. **Fall to** (began eagerly and hastely). 'The sailors eagerly *fell to* the homely food.'

Get

1. **Get at** (come near, reach). 'I could not *get at* him on account of the crowd.' 'Our object in this inquiry is to *get at* the truth.'

2. **Get ahead** (advance; prosper). 'Shanti *got ahead* of her brother in studies.'
3. **Get along** (proceed). 'We must manage to *get along* with our small means.'
4. **Get away** (leave; escape). 'I *got away* early from the meeting.'
5. **Get back** (recover; return). He tried to *get back* the money.' 'He *got back* safe to his house.'
6. **Get off** (1. alight from. 2. escape). 1. 'He *got off* with the money.' 2. 'He *got off* from the attack.'
7. **Get down** (descend). 'He *got down* from the platform.'
8. **Get forward** (advance). 'This is very discouraging to one who is trying to *get forward* in the world.'
9. **Get hold of** (seize). 'He has to *get hold of his* property.'
10. **Get in** (enter). 'Do not stand at the door, *get in*.'
11. **Get into** (enter; become involved into). 'They could not *get into* the house, as the doors were locked.' 'He has *got into* serious troubles.' 'This new reform is fast *getting into* favour with the people.'
12. **Get on** (progress; live together pleasantly). 'How is he *getting on* at the school?' 'The husband and wife cannot *get on* together.'
13. **Get out** (escape). 'He *got out* of the difficulty.'
14. **Get over** (overcome). 'I have *got over* my difficulties.'
15. **Get rid of** (free oneself from). 'He cannot *get rid of* drinking.'
16. **Get to** (reach). 'We have *got to* the end of the first book.'
17. **Get together** (assemble). 'They *got together* at the cinema hall.'
18. **Get through** (finish; pass through). 'He has *got through* half the work'. 'He is sure to *get through* the B. A. examination.'
19. **Get up** (1. rise from sleep. 2. prepare. 3. dress). 1. 'Children should *get up* early.' 2. '*Get up* some entertainment for these visitors.' 3. 'He *got up* like a prince.'
20. **Get loose** (become free). 'He *got loose* from constables.'

Give

1. **Give away** (give in charity or as gift). 'He *gave away* all his property to the poor.'
2. **Give in** (yield). 'Though defeated, he would not *give in*.'
3. **Give out** (emit; announce). 'Some flowers *give out* their richest fragrance at night.' 'He *gave out* that he was going to England.'

4. **Give over** (abandon). 'We should *give over* these useless activities.'
5. **Give rise to** (cause or produce). 'His conduct *gave rise* to grave suspicion.'
6. **Give up** (resign; cease from). 'He has *given up* smoking altogether.'
7. **Give vent to** (express). 'He *gave vent to* his grief in tears.'
8. **Give way** (break, yield to pressure). 'The bamboo *gave way* and the roof came down.' 'The old man *gave way* under his misfortunes and died of a broken heart.'

Go

1. **Go abroad** (go out of the country; become public). 'He is *going abroad* for a year.' 'A story *went abroad* to the effect that he had committed suicide by jumping into a well.'
2. **Go astray** (wander from the right course). 'They have *gone astray* from the path of virtue.'
3. **Go off** (1. depart. 2. be discharged). 1. 'He *went off* home.' 2. 'The gun would *go off*.'
4. **Go on** (proceed). 'Everything *went on* as usual.'
5. **Go out** (become extinguished). 'The light *went out*.'
6. **Go over** (1. read. 2. change sides). 1. 'I have *gone over* this book.' 2. 'He has *gone over* to the Socialist Party.'
7. **Go through** (suffer). 'If you knew I have *gone through*, you would pity me.'
8. **Go up** (increase). 'These days prices have *gone up* very high.'
9. **Go in for** (enter as a competitor; try to get; advocate). I will *go in for* the I. A. S. examination.' 'Do not *go in for* luxurious things in life.'

Hold

1. **Hold fast** (adhere to firmly). 'Honest men *hold fast* to their principles.'
2. **Hold on** (continue). 'I find it impossible to *hold on* any longer, and I must, therefore, resign my place.'
3. **Hold one's own** (maintain one's ground). 'I cannot *hold my own* against him in argument.'
4. **Hold out** (resist; not to yield). 'They *held out* against the enemy for six months.' 'I can *hold out* no prospect of promotion to you.'
5. **Hold together** (remain united). 'They will fail in their mission because they cannot *hold together*.'

6. **Hold up** (sustain; not to rain). 'His faith in God *held* him *up*, in the midst of all the troubles.' 'If the weather *holds up*, I shall be glad.'
7. **Hold over** (postpone). 'The High School Examination has been *held over* till Monday next.'
8. **Hold off** (keep at a distance). 'I love him very dearly; I cannot *hold him off*.'

Keep

1. **Keep back** (reserve or withhold). 'I will not *keep* it *back* from you.'
2. **Keep down** (hold under control). '*Keep down* your temper.'
3. **Keep from** (refrain from). 'He cannot *keep from* the use of tobacco.'
4. **Keep in** (restrain). 'He could not *keep in* his tears.'
5. **Keep off** (remain at a distance). 'Always *keep off* wicked people.' 'These curtains are meant to *keep off* mosquitoes.'
6. **Keep on** (continue to advance). 'In spite of difficulties, he *kept on* steadily.'
7. **Keep to** (adhere to; do according to). 'We should not *keep to* bad customs.' 'We should *keep to* our word'.
8. **Keep up** (maintain). 'It is not possible for everyone to *keep up* an elephant.' 'I will try to *keep up* the reputation of my family.'
9. **Keep up with** (not to fall behind). 'Can America *keep up with* Britain in the building of ships.'

Lay

1. **Lay by** (save for the future; put aside). 'One should *lay by* something for one's old age'. 'He has now *laid by* in other hobbies.'
2. **Lay bare** (expose). 'He *laid bare* all my secrets.'
3. **Lay before** (present to view). 'He *laid* his sad case *before* the Judge.'
4. **Lay in** (store). '*Lay in* provisions for winter.'
5. **Lay** oneself **down** (retire to rest; recline). 'He *laid* himself *down* on the soft grass.'
6. **Lay out** (1. expend. 2. put aside. 3. dress in gay clothes). '1. He *laid out* a thousand rupees in jewellery.' 2. 'He *laid out* all his ambitions'. 3. 'He *laid* himself *out*.'
7. **Lay up** (1. store. 2. confine to bed). *Lay up* for your treasures.' 'He is *laid up* with fever.'

8. **Lay under** (subject to). 'He has *laid* me *under* a great obligation.'
9. **Lay waste** (destroy or desolate). 'They *laid waste* the enemy's country with fire and sword.'

Look

1. **Look after** (take care of). 'He has one to *look after* him.'
2. **Look about** (be watchful). 'You have every need to *look about* you.' 'As they went along, they *looked about* for a good place on which to pitch their tent.'
3. **Look down upon** (despise) 'We should not *look down upon* the untouchables.'
4. **Look for** (1. expect. 2. search). 'I am *looking for* the arrival of the goods by the ship.' '*Look for* the key I lost yesterday.'
5. **Look into** (examine closely). 'When we *look not* the works of nature how marvellous is the evidence of skill and design.'
6. **Look on** (be a spectator). '*Look on* while we are playing the game.'
7. **Look out** (be on the watch). 'He is *looking out* for an opportunity of revenge.'
8. **Look over** (examine). '*Look over* these exercises.'
9. **Look to** (expect from). 'I shall *look to* you for payment.'
10. **Look through** (understand thoroughly). 'I must *look through* the case before giving my opinion.'
11. **Look up** (consult). 'He *looked up* the word in the dictionary.'
12. **Look upon** (regard; consider). 'He *looks upon* me as his brother.'

Make

1. **Make against** (injure). 'The circumstances will *make against* you in the case.'
2. **Make over** (transfer or give). 'He *made over* all his property to his sons.'
3. **Make away with** (destroy, kill; remove in an underhand manner). 'He *made away with* four thousand rupees.'
4. **Make for** (1. move towards. 2. to be advantageous to). 'The boat *made for* the shore.' 2. 'A war between India and Pakistan *will make for* the interest of the Great Powers.'
5. **Make much of** (to treat as much importance or value). 'He *made much of* his speech for the defence.'

6. **Make of** (1. understand. 2. esteem). 1. 'I do not know what to *make of* this letter.' 'He does not *make of* me more than a slave.'
7. **Make out** (1. understand. 2. prove). 1. 'I cannot *make out* why he comes to see me so often.' 2. 'He failed to *make out* his case.'
8. **Make up** (1. collect into a mass or sum. 2. adjust. 3. supply what is larking. 4. compose. 5. compensate. 6. determine). 1. '*Make up* a bundle.' 2. '*Make up* your quarrel.' 3. 'I want a rupee to *make up* the account.' 4. 'The book is *made up* of extract.' 5. 'He cannot *make up* his loss.' 6. '*Make up* your mind.'
8. **Make up for** (compensate). 'Her learning *makes up for* her want to beauty.'
9. **Make up to** (approach; try to win favour). 'He always *makes up to* rich people.'
10. **Make up with** (be reconciled with). 'I can never *make up with* him.'
11. **Make off with** (run away with). 'A thief broke into his house and *made off with* all his cash.'

Pass

1. **Pass through** (undergo). 'Great man *pass through* many difficulties.'
2. **Pass for** (to be regarded). 'He *passes for* a learned professor in our little community.'
3. **Pass away** (expire; die). 'His uncle *passed away* last night.'
4. **Pass over** (come and depart). 'A frown *passed over* his face as he read the letter.'

Put

1. **Put** (in) **across** (succeed in anything). 'I thought be would fail but he contrived to *put it across*.'
2. **Put by** (save). 'He *puts by* a little money'.
3. **Put down** (subdue). 'The rebellion was put down with great force'.
4. **Put forth** (exert). 'He *put forth* all his skill to defeat me.'
5. **Put in for** (offer oneself for). 'Several candidates have *put in for* the headmastership.'
6. **Put off** (postpone). 'Never *put off* till tomorrow what you can do today.'
7. **Put on** (1. wear. 2. assume). 1. 'He *put on* his coat.' 2. 'He *put on* an angry look.'

8. **Put out** (1. extinguish. 2. make angry. 3. disturb). 1. '*Put out* all the lights.' 2. He was very much *put out* by my conduct.' 3. 'This has *put out* all my arrangements.'
9. **Put up** (lodge or stay). 'These days he is *putting up* in the hostel.'
10. **Put up with** (submit to or tolerate; stay at a person). 'He could not *put up with* such an insult.' 'He is *putting up with* his uncle in his villa.'

Run

1. **Run after** (pursue; follow). 'He *ran after* the thief but could not catch him.'
2. **Run down** (speak disparagingly of). 'We must not *run* a man *down* simply because we do not like him.'
3. **Run high** (be violent). 'Party spirit was *running high* at that time.'
4. **Run on** (be continued). 'His account in my office has been *running on* for a year.'
5. **Run out** (come to an end). 'My leave has *run out*.' 'If land is cropped and not manured, it will soon *run out*.'
6. **Run over** (1. go over hastily. 2. overflew. 3. ride or drive over). 1. '*Run over* this book.' 2. 'The cup is *running over*.' 3. 'His car *ran over* a dog.'
7. **Run through** (1. waste money. 2. pierce). 1. 'He *ran through* his whole fortune in a year.' 2. 'His words *ran through* my heart.'
8. **Run up** (enlarge by additions). 'Your bill is *running up* fast.'

Set

1. **Set about** (begin). 'He *set about* his task with great enthusiasm.'
2. **Set aside** (1. reject. 2. leave out of account). 1. 'The judgment was *set aside*.' 2. *Setting* all other reasons *aside*, I can say.'
3. **Set in** (begin). 'The water has *set in*.'
4. **Set off** (1. start 2. show to advantage). 'They *set off* in search of the lion. The dress *sets off* her figure.'
5. **Set on** (instigate). 'He has been *set on* to do this.'
6. **Set out** (1. start on journey 2. display). 1. 'He *set out* on his travels.' 2. 'He *set out* his case with all the grace of a rhetorician.'
7. **Set forth** (exhibit). 'He *set forth* his views with cleverness and force.'
8. **Set up** (establish). 'It is difficult to *set up* world peace on a permanent basis.'

Stand

1. **Stand by** (support). 'I will *stand by* you in your troubles.'
2. **Stand out** (be prominent). 'The trees *stand out* against the dark sky.'
3. **Stand over** (be postponed). 'The matter must *stand over* for the present.'
4. **Stand to** (be consistent with). 'Her conduct does not *stand to* reason.'
5. **Stand up for** (defend; maintain). 'We are determined to *stand up for* our right.'
6. **Stand** (tolerate). 'I cannot *stand* this behaviour of yours.'

Strike

1. **Strike for** (start suddenly on a course for). 'The swimmer *struck for* the shore.'
2. **Strike off** (remove, as name from a list). 'His name was *struck off* the Attendance Register.'
3. **Strike up** (begin to play, said of musical instruments). 'The musicians were told to *strike up*.'
4. **Strike down** (attack). 'My friend is *struck down* with malaria.'
5. **Strike out** (devise). '*Strike out* some plan to finish this work as early as possible.'
6. **Strike in with** (agree with). 'His views *strike in with* yours.'

Take

1. **Take after** (resemble). 'He *takes after* his mother.'
2. **Takes down** (1. bring down from a height. 2. reduce to writing). 1. '*Take down* the flag.' 2. '*Take down* these notes.'
3. **Take for** (suppose to be). 'I *took him for* a drunkard.'
4. **Take in** (1. contract, 2. device. 3. comprise). 1. 'He *took in* that business.' 2. 'I cannot be *taken in* by his high–sounding words.' 3. 'The definition *took in* many things.'
5. **Take off** (mimic, copy in jest). 'He *takes off* his father's manner of walking.'
6. **Take to** (1. adopt the profession. 2. become addicted to). 1. 'My friend has *taken to* teaching.' 2. 'He has *taken to* smoking.'
7. **Take up** (occupy). 'It *takes up* much time to write a book on grammar.' 'These boxes *take up* a large space.'

8. **Taken aback** (surprised). 'He was *taken aback* when he came to know that all his jewels had been stolen.'

Throw

1. **Throw about** (fling here and there). 'We would not *throw about* our book.'
2. **Throw away** (lose by neglect) 'He has *thrown away* a fine opportunity.'

EXERCISES

Use the following expressions to form sentences:

1. To turn down
2. To put off
3. Look out
4. Look down upon
5. Turn up
6. Turn in
7. Cut off
8. See through
9. Set off
10. Take after
11. Tamper with
12. Tide over
13. Turn down
14. Wear out
15. Wind up
16. Pick out
17. Work up
18. Put out.

SOLUTIONS

1. I do not know why he *turned down* my request.
2. Never *put off* till tomorrow what you can do today.
3. He is *looking out* for an opportunity of revenge.
4. We should not *took down upon* the untouchables.

5. He will *turn up* tomorrow.
6. *Turn up* this ring.
7. The strike has been *called off*.
8. I *saw through* your trick and suspended you.
9. They *set off* in search of a lion.
10. He *takes after* his mother.
11. It is dangerous to *tamper with* gun powder.
12. A little money given to him would *tide over* all over his difficulties.
13. The Director has practically *turned down* his scheme.
14. His shoes are *worn out*.
15. He will *wind up* his discussion today.
16. You have *picked out* bad potatoes.
17. They will *work up* all these stones in binding the bridge.
18. The fire was *put out* soon.

IV. IDIOMATIC VERBIAL EXPRESSIONS

This chapter presents to the student a rich selection on idiomatic verbal expressions arranged in an alphabetical order. In the preceding chapter we explained and illustrated the phrases which are formed by the combination of appropriate prepositions with verbs. Here we shall study the phrases where the verb is joined with words of different parts of speech, mostly with nouns. A number of them are formed with the verb to be whereas other are made up with the verbs like *break, give, set, turn, through*, etc. Such verbal expressions as given here abound in good conversational English and the student will find instance of this in abundance in well-written novels or stories which largely reproduce or represent conversation as among well-educated people.

1. **To be up** (to be equal to; to be acquainted with). 'This main is *up to* all the tricks of the trade'.
2. **To be up and doing** (to be actively engaged). 'A farmer must be *up and doing* in spring if he would reap the harvest'.
3. **To be born with a silver spoon in one's mouth** (to be born in prosperous circumstances; to be a rich man's child). 'Those who are *born with a silver spoon in their mouth* rarely accomplish any of those great and good things which require force of character.'
4. **To be worth its weight in gold** (said of something extremely valuable). 'In the desert a bottle of water is often *worth its weight in gold*.'

5. **To be ill at ease** (to be disturbed in mind). A man is often *ill at ease* when he has to meet a superior and is uncertain how he may be received'.

6. **To be lost in the clouds** (is applied to a confused and confusing speaker whose thoughts are so hazy, so wrapped in clouds of metal confusion, that he cannot set forth his meaning clearly), 'Philosophers are often *lost in the clouds*'.

7. **To be all ears** (to be very attentive listener). 'I was *all ears* when he told me the story of his wife's elopement.'

8. **To be nobody** or **somebody** (to be a person of no importance or some importance). 'The Prime Minister is the real ruler and the Prince is a mere *nobody*.' 'He struts about with an air of importance as if he were *somebody*.'

9. **To be in one's cups** (to be drunk). 'It is dangerous to approach him when he is *in his cups*.'

10. **To be not fit to hold a candle to** (not to be named in comparison with). 'He is *not to hold a candle to* his predecessor.'

11. **To be weak** (or **vacant**) **in the upper storey** (to be crazy; feeble minded). 'How can I depend upon a man like him whose *upper storey is vacant*?'.

12. **To be under a cloud** (when a man rightly or wrongly falls under suspicion, he is said for the time being to be under a cloud; the sunshine of success or favour no longer falls upon him; he is not in good repute). 'The discovery of stolen goods in his house has brought him *under a cloud*.'

13. **To be under one's thumb** (to be unduly under one's rule or control). 'The King is absolutely *under the thumb* of his Prime Minister.'

14. **To be at daggers down** (said of two parties between whom there is as much bitter enmity as if they stood face to face with daggers drawn, ready to stab each other). 'The quarrel between these two men has unhappily grown more bitter now and they are *at daggers drawn.*'

15. **To be at a loss** (to be puzzled; to be unable to understand and decide). 'He is never *at a loss* for an appropriate world.'

16. **To be at a discount** (not to be demanded). 'Honestly is *at a discount* these days.'

17. **To be at one's wit's end** (to be greatly perplexed; not to know what to do in an emergency). 'He was *at his wit's end* when he saw the lion rushing towards him.'

18. **To be in bad** (or **good**) **odour** (to be the unpopular or popular). 'A man who is known to be of bad habits cannot be in *bad odour* with decent people.'

19. **To be at the helm of** (to be at the main position). 'He is *at the helm of* affairs.'

20. **To be beside oneself with grief** (or **joy**) (to be extremely grieved or happy). 'When he heard about the death of his friend, he was *beside himself with grief.*' 'I was *beside myself with joy* when I came to know that I was placed in the first division.'

21. **To be in a fix** (to be in perplexity). 'I am *in a fix* about that dacoit's threatening letter.'

22. **To be in petty pass** (to be in a difficulty). 'When I saw the lion rushing towards me, I was *in petty pass,* and did not know what to do.'

23. **To be in keeping with** (to be suitable to; harmonize with). 'The simple kindly act is quite *in keeping with* his character.'

24. **To be in a person's good books** (to be in favour with a person; the opposite is, to be in a person's bad books). 'His brilliant success at the examination has led him *to be in the good books* of the Principal.'

25. **To be in one's teens** (a person is said to be in his teens when he is between the age of twelve and twenty, all the numbers coming in between end in teems). 'In England, few girls are married while still *in their teens.*'

26. **To be in tune** (a person is said to be in tune for a thing when he is in the mood to take it readily or generally to be in a happy state of mind). 'Are you *in tune* for study today?'

27. **To be in the swim** (to be in the main current of water). 'It is very difficult for a man *to be in the swim* of modern society, for he cannot afford to give dinners and parties to others.'

28. **To be one's last legs** (to be in a tottering or sinking condition; to be about to collapse). 'In some sections of the Hindu community, the caste systems is *on its last legs.*'

29. **To be out of sorts** (to be slightly unwell). 'I have been *out of sorts* today and not up to my work at all.'

30. **To be the order of the day** (to be the prevent fashion or custom) 'Renovation and improvement are the *order of the day.*'

31. **To be at loggerheads** (to be at strife). 'The two friends are now *at loggerheads.*'

32. **To bear the brunt of** (to endure the main force or shock of). 'The centre of the army has to *bear the brunt of* the battle.'
33. **To be on the wane** (to be gradually growing less to be diminishing). 'The power of the Turkish Empire had long *been on the wane.*'
34. **To beat the air** (to make efforts that are vain, useless, fruitless). 'His speech merely *beat the air*; there was no cogency in his argument.'
35. **To beggar description** (beyond one's power to describe adequately). 'The beauty of Taj Mahal *beggars description.*'
36. **To believe one's ears** (or **eyes**). 'You will scarcely *believe your ears* when I tell you that there are some countries where the sun does not set for six months on end.' 'I could not *believe my eyes* when I saw my long-lost dog turning towards me.'
37. **To bell the cat** (to render a common enemy harmless of evil at great personal risk. The phrase is taken from a well-known fable—A cat made herself a terror to a number of mice, one of whom suggested that a bell should be tied round the neck of the cat to give them warning of her approach. They all agreed to this suggestion. Thereupon an old mouse exclaimed, "But who will be the cat?" (it being a venturesome and risky job). 'All can boast of their bravery, but very few can *bell the cat.*'
38. **To bid fair to** (to be likely to give fair prospect of). 'His health is so good that be *bids fair* to live till he is sixty.'
39. **To blow one's own trumpet** (to speak highly of one's own deeds). 'I don't like to talk to him; he is always *blowing his own trumpet.*'
40. **To break the ice** (to overcome obstacles and make a beginning to commence a conversation where there has been an awkward silence). 'For several minutes they sat without exchanging a word but at last one of them *broke the ice* by making an observation on the weather.'
41. **To bring down the house** (to call forth general and loud applause). 'On the very first night to her appearance on the stage she *brought down the house with the house* with her excellent acting.'
42. **To break the news to a person** (to communicate unexpected bad news to a man in such a way as to diminish the shock). 'He *broke the news* his wife as gently as he could that he had lost all his fortune through the failure of the bank.'
43. **To burn the candle at both ends** (to overspend one's energies so as to injure one's health, or to spend money lavishly). 'He will soon come to grief for he is *burning the candle at both ends.*'

44. **To bury the hatchet** (to make peace, the 'hatchet', referred to in the phrase, was a weapon used by North American Indian. When tribes of these people who had been at war, made peace, it was a custom among them that their leaders should sit down together and all smoke in turn from the same pipe, called the 'pie of peace'). 'In his appeal to Hindus and Muslims, Mahatma Gandhi advised them to *bury the hatchet* and harmony in the land.'

45. **To call a spade a spade** (to speak in plain terms, to describe things by their correct names). 'Such acts amount to a crime against established Government; we must *call a spade a spade* and not describe such deeds as patriotic actions.'

46. **To change hands** (property is said to change hands when it passes from one owner to another either by sale, or gift, or in any other way). 'This house has changed hands twice in the last ten years.' 'There were pickpockets in the crowd and several watches *changed hands*.'

47. **To carry matters with a high hand** (to domineer; to take strong measures to exercise authority with crushing force). 'The Principal of the college *carried matters with a high hand* and expelled two students for what after all was but a trivial offence.'

48. **To cast (put, throw) into the shade** (to make something less attractive or less remarkable). 'Tennyson's great personality *cast into the shade all other poets of his age*.'

49. **To pour oil on troubled waters** (to make the situation calm). 'The two brothers exchanged hot words but the intervention of their mother *poured oil on troubled waters*.'

50. **To catch a Tartar** (to catch or encounter an adversary who proves too strong for his assailant. A Tartar is a native of Tartary. The story goes that in battle with the Turksan Irish soldier shouted to his comrade, 'I have caught, a Tartar.' 'Then bring him with you.' *i.e.*, as prisoner. 'But he won't let come.' 'Then come alone yourself.' 'But he won't let me.' The fact was that the Tartar had caught the Irish man. Hence the general meaning of the phrase as given above). 'Akbar soon found out that he had *caught a Tartar in* Rana Pratap.'

51. **To cast a slur upon one** (to cast a slight reproach upon one by word or act). 'He promised not to do anything which would *cast a slur upon* the fair name of his parents.'

52. **To clip one's wings** (to deprive one of power, to render one weak or ineffective. 'The minister is ambitious, but the Prince will *clip his wings*.'

53. **To come home to a person** (to appeal successfully to his reason or his self-interest, to touch his feelings closely). 'Soon it *came home to me* that I was not fit for the post.'

54. **To come a standstill** (to come to a stop or standing at rest). 'When the car *came to a standstill* for want of petrol, the chief left it there and made his way in a tonga.'

55. **To come off with flying colours** (to come out from a conflict with brilliant success). 'The claimant was beaten when his case was first tried, but he appealed to higher court and now he has *come off with flying colours.*'

56. **To cross one's mind** (to occur to one). 'He was just starting out when it *crossed his mind* that he left his purse on the table.'

57. **To cry for the moon** (to desire an impossible thing). 'Your hope of being married with the Magistrate's daughter is simply *crying for the moon.*'

58. **To cry from the housetop** (to announce publicly). 'He *cries from the housetop* that his uncle is a rogue of the first water.'

59. **To curry favour** (to seek to win favour be gifts or flattery). 'It is obvious that by your present of fruits, you are only trying to *curry favour* with him.'

60. **To do a thing off hand** (to do it at once, without delay or hesitation, and with ease and without preparation). 'I gave him a difficult problem in Mathematics and he *did it off hand.*'

61. **To dig the grave of one's reputation** (to do something which would end one's good name and reputation). 'By taking part in the strike *he dug the grave of his reputation.*'

62. **To die in harness** (to continue to the last in one's business or profession). 'It was his constant prayer that he might *die in harness.*'

63. **To do things under the rose** (to do it secretly; among the ancients the rose as a symbol of secrecy was hung up at entertainments, to indicate that nothing said there was to be disclosed). 'The two lovers performed their marriage *under the rose.*'

64. **To draw the line somewhere** (to set some limit). 'I cannot allow him to go on in his immoral ways, I have to *draw the line somewhere.*'

65. **To end in smoke** (said of efforts that come to nothing). 'He made a great fuss about having an investigation, but it all *ended in smoke.*'

66. **To eat humble pie** (to humiliate oneself). 'The millowner thinks that the strikers will soon *eat humble pie* and return to their work.'

67. **To face the music** (to face trouble). 'The thief who stole my furniture is now *facing the music*.'

68. **To fan the flame** (to increase an evil influence, as sedition, agitation, passion, excitement. **To add fuel to the flame** is to add fresh provocation, intensify strong feeling or passion). 'Openly the professed loyalty, but in secret he was *fanning the flame* of sedition.' 'Unless effect crush the rebellion only *added fuel to the flame*.'

69. **To fall flat** (to have no effect). 'All my words of advice *fell flat* upon him.'

70. **To fall a prey to** (to be the victim of). 'Sometimes even educated people *fall a prey* to superstitious beliefs.'

71. **To feather one's nest** (to provide for oneself especially from property not one's own; the phrase implies dishonesty). 'These days our ministers are busy *feathering their own nests* without caring for the interest of the nation.'

72. **To feel the pulse** (to find out the secret opinions). 'The Prime Minister sometimes makes an important statement in Parliament in order that through the comments made on it in the public press he may *feel the pulse* of the nation.'

73. **To feel one's way** (to proceed cautiously so as to avoid risks and dangers). 'A man starting a new business should *feel his way* carefully for some time.'

74. **To fight shy of** (to attempt to avoid a thing or a person). 'I *fight shy of* air travel because the movement makes me sick.'

75. **To fight to the bitter end** (to carry on a contest careless of the consequences). 'The two parties were determined to *fight to the bitter end*.'

76. **To find one's feet** (to grow familiar with new conditions; to feel at home in new surroundings). 'The little boy felt very strange at the new school, but in a couple of weeks he *found his feet* and settled down.'

77. **To fish in troubled waters** (to make personal profit out of a disturbance). 'When two communities fight with each other, a third generally tries to *fish in troubled waters* of communalism.'

78. **To flog a dead horse** (to revive interest in a subject which is out of date and has already been discussed threadbare). 'There is no use *flogging a dead horse*.'

79. **To gain ground** (to succeed slowly). 'His arguments *gained ground* and he won the case.'

80. **To get into a mess** (to drift into difficulties; to get into a middle). 'His accounts seem to have *got into a mess*.'

81. **To get the upper hand** (to get the better or superior position). 'Of the two rival spinning companies, one is richer and better managed than the other, and therefore, soon *gets the upper hand.*'

82. **To get into hot water** (to be in perplexing, difficult and irritating circumstances). 'The schoolmaster *got into hot water* for taking part in political meetings.'

83. **To give broad side** (to make a vigorous attack upon an opponent, to attack with a volley of arguments). 'I bore with his insolence as long down his head for shame.'

84. **To give the devil his due** (to give credit to bad man for his good actions). 'No doubt, he is a quarrelsome fellow, but to *give the devil his due* he is honest and diligent.'

85. **To give someone a bit of your mind** (to scold him, to find fault with him, to speak or write upbraidingly to him). 'He has treated me very badly, and I want to write a letter and *give him a bit of my mind.*'

86. **To give or show a person the cold shoulder** (to treat him coldly; to receive him without cordiality). 'How hateful it is for a man to *give the cold shoulder* to his former friends because he has now grown richer than they.'

87. **To give currency to** (to make current, to make publicly known). 'It is wicked *to give currency* to false and scandalous news.'

88. **To give quarter to** (to have sympathy with). 'Generous persons always *give quarter to* the poor and afflicted.'

89. **To go a long way** (to go far, to be nearly sufficient for). 'The newspapers *went a long way* in criticizing the Government.'

90. **To go out of one's way to do a thing** (to deviate from one's ordinary course of conduct in order to do something). 'You should be willing *to go out of your way* to oblige a friend.'

91. **To go hot and cold** (to have excess of shame). 'She *went hot and cold* when the name of her secret lover was mentioned.'

92. **To go with tail between the legs** (to go with a beaten cowardly look as a defeated dog does). 'He was speaking high of truth and honesty but when I reached there and reminded him of his past sinful life he *went away with his tail between his legs.*'

93. **To grease the plam** (to bribe). 'In some departments there is so much of corruption that you cannot get anything done unless you *grease the plam* of the officials.'

94. **To have all one's eggs in one basket** (to risk all one's goods in the same venture). 'It is not wise to *have all one's eggs in one basket.*

EXERCISES

Use the following expressions in sentences:

1. Through thick and thin
2. off and on
3. The alpha and omega
4. Tooth and nail

SOLUTIONS

1. Pt. Kamalapati Tripathi followed Mrs. Indira Gandhi *through thick and thin.*
2. I have been going there *off and on.*
3. *The Alpha and Omega* of Mahatma Gandhi's life was to improve the lot of the untouchables.
4. He opposed me *tooth and nail.*

V. MISCELLANEOUS IDIOMATIC EXPRESSIONS

These are some commonly used expressions in English and deserve the study and attention of every student.

1. **Once in a blue moon** (on rare occasions). 'I see a film *once in a blue moon*.'
2. **In the blues** (melancholy and low-spirited). 'There is nothing better than the company of young and playful children for a person who is *in the blues*.'
3. **The die is cast** (final decision has been taken). 'Once the *die is cast*, there is no going back.'
4. **Helter skelter** (in haste and confusion). 'as the riot broke out' shops were hurriedly closed and people ran *helter skelter*.'
5. **From pillar to post** (from one place of shelter to another). 'These days graduates run *from pillar to post* in search of employment, finding nothing but disappointment.'
6. **In the teeth of opposition** (in spite of bitter opposition). 'Without minding dangers in his way, he proceeded on *in the teeth of opposition* and won his point.'
7. **Willy nilly** (whether he wishes or not). '*Willy nilly*, he has to go there.'
8. **Out of the wood** (free from danger or difficulty). 'Even speaks of gravity of employment in India but very few suggests a way *out of the wood*.'

9. **That cock won't fight** (that plan will not work). 'The student wanted to pass the examination by unfair means but he was caught red-handed by the invigilator and his *cock did not fight*.'
10. **The last nail in the coffin** (the last event which brings about the complete end of something). 'The communal policy of Aurangzeb put *the last nail in the coffin* of Mughal Empire.'
11. **An eye-wash** (a pretence). 'He is a selfish man and his help to you seems to me a mere *eye-wash*.'
12. **Next to nothing** (almost nothing). 'The rats have attacked the bread and there is *next to nothing* left.'
13. **Like a fish out of water** (not to be in congenial surroundings). 'The teacher felt *like a fish out of water* for he knew very little about the subject on which he was speaking.'
14. **There are wheels within wheels** (when it is found that a difficult business is more complicated than we had supposed, we say). '*There are wheels within wheels* just as in very complicated machinery, wheels sometimes work within other wheels.' (The saying is used metaphorically when there are hidden complications in a scheme.)
15. **A gentleman at large** (a pretentious and unreliable person). 'Beware of persons who are *gentleman at large*.'
16. **By dint of** (by virtue of). 'Success in life is achieved *by dint of* honest industry.'
17. **Up to the mark** (up to the proper standard). 'His answer is not *up to the mark*.'
18. **The chances are** (the likelihood is). 'If you give a knife to a baby, *the chances are* that he will cut himself.'
19. **Between the cup and the lip** (on the point of achievement). 'There is many a slip *between the cup and the lip*.'
20. **No wonder the** (nothing surprising). 'Since he is such a great favourite of the Prime Minister, *no wonder that* he may become a Governor.'
21. **A wolf in sheep's clothing** (a dangerous person who pretends to be harmless). 'Don't believe him; he is a *wolf in sheep's clothing*.'
22. **Fish** (doubtful). 'I don't like that. It sounds a bit *fishy* to me.'
23. **A windfall** (an unexpected good fortune). 'Shylock had a *windfall* and suddenly became rich.'
24. **Out of gear** (in disorder). 'During the Civil War, the Government of the country was *out of gear* for a pretty long time.'

VI. SOME COLLOQUIAL IDIOMATIC SENTENCES

English is a living language and changes with the times. Here are some colloquial phrases, constructions and expressions. Study them closely:

1. His days are numbered.
2. He's got a screw loose.
3. Nothing is too bad for him to do, he can commit all the sins in the calendar.
4. He is a harmless soul.
5. He never grows weary in well-doing.
6. What a chatter-box she was!
7. Who ever had thing all his own way.
8. Willy nilly we have to do it.
9. It is only a one-horse business.
10. It cost me no end of money.
11. He's rather off colour today.
12. If the cap fits, wear it.
13. That will put his nose out of point.
14. Out with it, or I shall be the death of you.
15. He was laughing up his sleeve.
16. I don't care a fig for him.
18. By Jove! You are a fine fellow.
19. Get along! If you wait for him, you will wait till Doomsday.
20. When he saw the money-lender, his heart sank into his boots.
21. A mountain in labour produces in a mouse.
22. The book is selling like hot cakes.
23. He could not contain himself for joy.
24. It is never expected that you would give me the cold shoulder at the time of need.
25. He is always ringing his own bell.
26. He is a villain of the deepest eye.
27. You are teaching an old woman to dance.
28. He is a mere turn-coat.
29. He has eaten me out of house and home.

30. He is a mere figure head.
31. You have been hiding your light under bushel.
32. His wits have gone a wool gathering.
33. Where there is peace, there is no need of judge.
34. Let them bathe my soul in the beauty of sunset.

EXERCISES

Frame sentences from the following idioms:

1. a. From hand to mouth.
   b. Fish out of the water.
   c. To let the cat out of the bag.
   d. To see eye to eye.
   e. In his true colours.
   f. In someone's good books.
2. a. Turn the corner.
   b. Cut a poor figure.
   c. The grapes are sour.
   d. The bold facts.
   e. Play the second fiddle.
   f. The eleventh hour.
   g. For a rainy day.
   h. From pillar to post.
3. a. To have an axe to grind.
   b. To play fast and loose.
   c. To show a clean pair of heels.
   d. To fight sky of
   e. To be at loggerheads

Mark the correct meaning of the idioms from the alternative given below:

1. Will–o'–the wisp:
   a. to cut in a childish way
   b. acting in a foolish way

c. to have desires unbacked by effort
d. anything which eludes or deceives
e. yearning of the spirit.

2. A snake in the grass:
   a. a secret or hidden enemy
   b. not reliable person
   c. very ferocious snake
   d. unrecognizable danger
   e. unforeseen happening
3. To look down one's nose at:
   a. to show anger
   b. to backbite
   c. to insult in the presence of others
   d. to regard with half-hidden displeasure or contempt
   e. none of these
4. Hobson's choice:
   a. excellent choice
   b. no choice at all because there is one thing to take or do
   c. choice to live or die
   d. big man's choice
   e. first choice
5. To have a chip or one's shoulder:
   a. to have deep cut would on the shoulder
   b. to be deserving of piece
   c. to have a defiant air
   d. to be boastful
   e. signs on the shoulder showing timidity
6. To meet one's Waterloo:
   a. to die fighting
   b. to die an ignoble death
   c. to meet one's final death
   d. to meet a strong adversary
   e. to meet with humiliation

7. To flog a dead horse:
   a. to do a vain thing
   b. to try to table work from a weak horse
   c. to beat a horse that is dead
   d. to revive interest in a subject which is out of date
   e. to act in a foolish way
8. To be lost in the cloud:
   a. to be concealed from the view.
   b. to find oneself in a very uncomfortable position
   c. to be perplexed
   d. to fly deep in the clouds
   e. to meet with one's. death
9. To fish in troubled waters:
   a. to indulge in evil conspiracies
   b. to aggravate the situation
   c. to be perplexed
   d. to catch fish in disturbed waters
   e. to make the most of a bad bargain
10. To take the wind out of another's sails:
    a. to defect the motives of another
    b. to cause harm to another
    c. to anticipate another and to gain advantage over him
    d. to manoeuvre to mislead another on the high seas
    e. none of these
11. To wrangle over an ass's shadow:
    a. to do something funny
    b. to quarrel over the possession of an ass.
    c. to waste time on pretty things
    d. to quarrel over trifles
    e. to act in a foolish way
12. To fly off the handle:
    a. to dislocate
    b. to be indifferent

c. to lose one's temper

d. to be air borne

e. to act in a way unmindful of consequences

13. To bring one's eggs to a bad market:

a. to fail in one's plans because one goes to the wrong people for help

b. to bring one's commodities to a market where these is no demand for them

c. to show one's talents before audience which is incapable of appreciating them

d. to face a humiliating situation

e. to act when the opportunity is lost

VII. PARONYMS

Broadly speaking, paronyms are the words which are similar in form of derivation but different in meaning of use.

1. **Alternate** ('being by turns' or 'of thin of two kinds coming each after one of the other kind') 'The doctor sees the patient on *alternate* days.' 'Boys and girls will step forward *alternately (i.e.,* a boy, then a girl, then a boy, and so on).'
   Alternative (one of the two courses or things between which there is a choice). 'There is no *alternative*, he must go to jail.'
2. **Acceptance** (the act of accepting a thing). 'I was glad at his *acceptance* of my invitation.'
   Acceptation (the interpretation put on something). 'There are several *acceptations*' of the word 'romantic'.
3. **Accession** (mean 'actual coming to', so *accession* to the throne—coming to the throne, *i.e.,* becoming sovereign). 'His *accession* to the throne has not yet taken place.'
   Access (means the possibility of 'coming to' so *access* to the throne—the opportunity of coming to the throne *i.e.,* approaching the sovereign). 'His *access* to fortune was barred.' 'He has no *access* to the Principal.'
4. **Accessary** (involves the idea of intentional aid or consent and is accordingly used with reference to persons and their actions). 'He was an *accessary,* if not the leader in the crime.' 'This course of action has made us *accessary* to the crime.'
   Accessory (has no such implication of consent, and is applied chiefly to things). 'These are the *accessory* details of the picture.'

5. **Act** (the thing done). 'I am thankful to you for this *act* of kindness.'
   Action (the doing of a thing). 'We should be sincere in our speech and *action*.'
6. **Admission** (being admitted). 'His *admission* to the class was provisional.'
   Admittance (getting in). 'He was not allowed *admittance* into the Principal's room.'
7. **Artist** (one who has to do with a fine art). 'A poet is not less an *artist* than a painter.'
   Artiste (a performer in singing, dancing etc.). 'The opera company consisted of a dozen *artistes*.'
   Artisan (one who practices some handicraft). 'The *artisans* of Kashmir are generally efficient and skilful.'
8. **Artistic** (beautiful, or having aesthetic powers). 'It is a very *artistic* design.'
   Artful (cunning, clever). 'He achieved success by *artful* means.'
   Artificial (is opposed to natural). 'Town life is *artificial*.'
9. **Appropriateness** (suitability). 'The works of Tagore are noted for their *appropriateness* in style.'
   Appropriation (making one's own). 'The *appropriation* of all his property by his friend is a clear proof of avarice.'
10. **Affecting** (moving, touching, pathetic). 'This film is full of many *affecting* scenes and situations.'
    Affectation (false display, forced imitation, insincere pretence). 'He always speaks with great pose and *affectation*.'
11. **Beside** (by the side of, close to). 'At the function I sat *beside* the president.'
    Besides (moreover, in addition to). '*Besides* helping me with money. He gave me some books also.'
12. **Barbarian** (of the primitives). 'A *barbarian* king—a king of barbarians.' 'A *barbarian* custom—a custom among barbarians.'
    Barbaric (is used in a favourable sense and means (simple, unsophisticated, rough). 'I like his *barbaric* simplicity.'
    Barbarous (is used in an unfavourable sense and means cruel, inhuman). 'War is altogether a *barbarous* business.'
13. **Beneficial** (useful, advantageous). 'Primary education will prove *beneficial* to the people of this country.'
    Beneficent (kind, generous). 'Let us be charitable and *beneficent* to the poor.'

14. **Confident** (to be sure, certain). 'You can be never *confident* of your success.'
Confidant (one who is entrusted with a secret). 'He is a treacherous fellow, you should not make him your *confidant*.'

15. **Completeness** (perfection). 'No writer can claim *completeness* in style.'
Completion (ending). 'I shall give your wages on the *completion* of the work.'

16. **Ceremonious** (Particular in observing forms; implies formalities overdone). 'His greeting was too *ceremonious*.'
Ceremonial (relating to ceremony and rites). 'Diwali and Dashehra are *ceremonial* occasions.'

17. **Contemptible** (deserving contempt). 'His conduct was highly *contemptible*.'
Contemptuous (hateful, disdainful, expressing contempt). 'He dismissed the servant with a *contemptuous* gesture.'

18. **Comprehensible** (extensive, including all the aspects). 'The book gives us a *comprehensive* survey of the present state of international affairs.'
Comprehensible (capable of being understood). 'His ideas on the subject are very clear and *comprehensible*.'

19. **Considerable** ('much', moderately 'large'). 'I have spent a *considerable* amount of money upon the education of my son.'
Considerate (thoughtful, regardful of others' interest). Being a *considerate* man, he always looks to the comfort of others.'

20. **Continuous** (implies that continuity is absolute and uninterrupted that there are no breaks). 'It rained *continuously* for three days (*i.e.*, without stopping).'
Continual (implies that there are occasional breaks). 'The dog kept up a *continual* barking (*i.e.*, barked with occasional breaks now and then).'

21. **Corporal** (means of human body). 'The crime you have committed deserves *corporal* punishment.'
Corporeal (means of the nature of body, material, tangible). 'Saints do not care much for *corporeal* pleasures.'

22. **Continuance** (duration, or time of remaining). 'He will draw the bonus during his *continuance* in the service.'
Continuation (prolongation or resumption). 'The *continuation* of the work delayed long than necessary.'

23. **Childish** (used in a bad means silly, trifling). 'He is a grown up man but his habits are *childish*.'
Child-like (used in a good sense and means as simple and innocent as a child). 'His *child-like* simplicity pleases everyone.'

24. **Dependent** (is an adjective meaning 'relying on'). 'Good men are always *dependent* on their own powers.'
Dependant (is a noun meaning one who depends on others for one's maintenance). 'I have a large number of *dependants* to look after.'

25. **Dependence** (reliance; living at another's cost). '*Dependence* on self is the only way to success, and *dependence* on God is the only salvation.'
Dependency (subject country). 'India is no longer a *dependency* of England.'

26. **Disinterested** ((unselfish; free from prejudice and personal motive). 'Mahatma Gandhi rendered *disinterested* service to India and her people.'
Uninterested (indifferent; lacking in interest). 'He is altogether *uninterested* in these affairs.'

27. **Distinctness** (clearness). '*Distinctness* of speech is essential in a teacher.'
Distinction (honour). 'It is a matter of rare *distinction* to become a Fellow of Royal Society.'

28. **Divers** (several or sundry). '*Divers* men tried to solve the problem.' '*Divers* plans were suggested.'
Diverse (markedly different or unlike). 'Their views were as *diverse* as London and Paris.'

29. **Deliverance** (rescue, emancipation, freedom). 'What can bring about the *deliverance* of man from the bondage of sin, sorrow and suffering?'
Delivery (uttering of speech; handing over of letters or goods). 'His speech was as remarkable for its ideas for its *delivery*'. 'I want an immediate *delivery* of this letter, you should at once start with it.'

30. **Device** (noun; a plan). 'It was a building of rare *device*.'
Devise (verb; to plan). '*Devise* a way out of this difficulty.'

31. **Decided** (definite). 'I gave him a *decided* answer.'
Decisive (that which ends a discussion or controversy finally). 'The first Battle of Panipat was a *decisive* one.'

32. **Depositary** (one with whom anything is deposited, trustee). 'He is the trusted *depositary* of the ornaments of the widow.'
Depository (a storehouse). 'Literature is the immortal *depository* of the best that has been thought in the world.'

33. **Destination** (goal; the place where we have to reach). 'My *destination* is Bombay.'
Destiny (fate). 'Teachers are the architects of the *destiny* of their country'.

34. **Enviable** (means arousing envy). 'His *enviable* position makes any people jealous of him.'
Envious (means feeling envy). 'We should not be *envious* of neighbour's progress.'

35. **Effective** (means having a high degree of effect). 'The medicine he took was *effective*.'
Effectual (applies to action, and means not falling short of the complete effect aimed at). 'The means he adopted were *effectual* (produced the desired effect).'
Efficacious (means 'sure to have the desired effect.'; it is used of things, principally medicines). 'Quinine proves *efficacious* in malarial fever.' 'He did the work *efficaciously*.'

36. **Envelop** (is a noun meaning a letter-cover). 'Correspondence with the Secretary should be done only is sealed *envelopes*.'
Envelop (is a verb meaning to cover, surround or wrap round). 'The entire atmosphere was *enveloped* in darkness.'

38. **Especial** (means 'to an exceptional degree'). 'The weather has been *especially* cold lately.'
Special (means 'for one purpose and no other'). 'He came *specially* for this meeting.' He made a *special* announcement.'

39. **Elemental** (pertaining to the elements). 'The ship sailed ashore in spite of *elemental* difficulties. (*i.e.,* wind and storm, etc.)
Elementary (rudimentary, introductory). '*Elementary* education is compulsory in all progressive countries.'

40. **Estimate** (approximate valuation of a thing). 'The engineer submitted to the Municipal Board an *estimate* of proposed construction.'
Estimation (opinion; judgement). 'Sri J. L. Nehru was held in high *estimation* by all politicians.'

41. **Exceptional** (rare; unusual). 'Abraham Lincoln was a man of *exceptional* abilities.'
Exceptionable (objectionable). 'His speech was condemned as it was full of *exceptionable* remarks.'

42. **Exposure** (being exposed to air, cold, etc) 'Protect the patient from *exposure* otherwise he will catch cold.'
Exposition (explanation). 'Tilak's *exposition* of the Bhagwat Gita is incomparable.'

43. **Economic** (associated only with economy). 'First we have to improve the *economic* conditions of our countrymen.'
Economical (associated with economy; frugal; thrifty). 'He is very *economical* in his habits.'

44. **Formalism** (habitual observances of rules or rites). '*Formalism* is not religion; just as the body is not the soul.'
Formality (ceremony; show). 'You need not observe *formalities* with my friend.'

45. **Fatal** (deadly). 'He received a *fatal* wound in his arm.'
Fatalist (one who believes in fate). 'Indians are generally *fatalists.*'
Fateful (important; producing important results). 'World War II was a *fateful* event in the history of the world.'

46. **Forceful** (possessing force). 'He has a *forceful* personality.'
Forcible (done by force or compulsion). 'The police made a *forcible* entry.'

47. **Godly** (pious). 'Jesus Christ led a *godly* life.'
God-like (resembling God). 'To many Indians mahatma Gandhi was a *God-like* man.' 'The *God-like* prince administered equal justice to the rich and the poor.'

48. **Graceful** (handsome). 'She has a *graceful* appearance.'
Gracious (merciful). 'God save our *gracious* king.' 'God is *gracious.*'

49. **Human** (belonging to mankind). 'Self-interest is deeply ingrained in *human* nature.'
Humane (kind; merciful). 'The animals are treated under *humane* conditions.'

50. **Honorary** (holding office without any remuneration or pay). 'He was appointed an *honorary* professor.'
Honourable (worthy of honour). 'His father is an *honourable* man of this town.'

51. **Healthy** (means enjoying health). 'Meat-eaters are not always *healthy*.'
Healthful (means preserving or promoting health). 'Egg is a *healthful* diet.'

52. **Historic** (famous or likely to become famous in history). 'Agra is a *historic* place.'
Historical (pertaining to history). 'Walter Scott wrote *historical novels*.'

53. **Imaginary** (fancied, unreal). 'The Equator is an *imaginary* line round the world.'
Imaginative (given to imagining; contemplative). 'Only those writers who possess *imaginative* faculties can produce original works.'

54. **Industrious** (diligent, laborious). 'There is nothing difficult in the world for an *industrious* man.'
    Industrial (relating to industry or commerce). 'Kanpur is an *industrial* centre.'
55. **Intelligent** (wise, sensible). 'She is an *intelligent* girl.' 'He made an *intelligent* statement.'
    Intelligible (clear and understandable). 'His speech was not *intelligible* to many.'
56. **Judicial** (pertaining to legal justice, or to a judge). 'There ought to be a *judicial* enquiry into his case.'
    Judicious (prudent, wise). 'Our Principal is a man of kind and *judicious* nature.'
57. **Kind** (refers to persons as well as to acts and feelings, and means tender, compassionate). 'He is a *kind* man.'
    Kindly (refers to acts and feelings and means benevolent, gracious). 'Such *kindly* acts of sympathy and affection win us fame.'
58. **Loudly** (in a loud voice). 'Do not speak so *loudly* in the reading room of the library.'
    Aloud (in an audible voice). 'He spoke *aloud* so that everyone present in the hall might listen to him.'
59. **Luxuriant** (is used to express richness in growth). 'Her hair is *luxuriant*.' 'There is a *luxuriant* growth of flowers in my friend's garden.'
    Luxurious (implies luxury or fashion). 'After his father's death he led a very *luxurious* life and soon came to grief.'
60. **Lovable** (worthy of love). 'He possesses many *lovable* qualities.' 'He is a *lovable* figure among his friends.'

VIII. HOMONYMS

We might misuse words not simply because they are similar in meaning or form but also because they sometimes happen to be similar in their sound or pronunciation. Such words as are similar in sound, though different in meaning are properly called homonyms. Identify and collect more such words apart from this list below.

1. **Accede** (agree). 'He has *acceded* to my request.'
   Exceed (surpass; to be greater). 'Write an essay not *exceeding* four pages.'
2. **Access** (approach; reach; admittance). 'Everyone should have an *access* to the place of religious worship.'
   Excess (superabundance; more than due). '*Excess* of everything is bad.'

3. **Accept** (take). 'He *accepted* my presents with thanks.'
   Except (leaving out). 'You cannot say that every Congressman *except* Sri Nehru was corrupt.'
4. **Adapt** (suit; accommodate to). 'One should *adapt* oneself to whatever circumstances one is placed in.'
   Adept (expert; skilful. 'He is an *adept* in the art of public speaking.'
   Adopt (take up). 'I have not yet decided which course of life I should *adopt*.'
5. **Affect** (1. to pretend, 2. to act upon). 'He *affects* to much ignorance.' 'The famine *affected* a large part of the district.'
   Effect (as verb it means 'accomplish', or carry into practice; as noun, it means 'result'). 'He *effected* his plans by hard labour.' 'Cinema-films produce a bad *effect* on the youth of our country.'
6. **Addition** (putting more). 'Will you have some snacks in *addition* to tea?'
   Edition (a number of books printed at one time). 'The first *edition* of his book sold like hot cakes.'
7. **Alter** (change). 'Nothing can *alter* my opinion about him.'
   Altar (place of offering in a temple or church). 'In Indian temples incense is burnt at the *altar*.' 'He died at the *altar* of freedom.'
8. **Allusion** (indirect reference). 'We looked at each other wondering which of us he was *alluding* to.' 'This poem is full of *allusions.*'
   Illusion (a deceptive appearance). 'Vedantists regard the material world as an *illusion*.'
9. **Apposite** (proper; suitable). 'He made in his speech some very *apposite* remarks on the present system of education in our country.'
   Opposite (standing in front or contrary). 'There is a small house *opposite* the office-building.'
10. **Assent** (agreement; concurrence). 'He gave his *assent* to the proposal.'
    Ascent (going up). 'The *ascent* to the Himalayas is a difficult task.'
11. **Antic** (odd, strange). 'His gestures are *antic*.'
    Antique (ancient; old-fashioned). 'He is very fond of collecting *antique* coins.'
12. **Assay** (1. attempt. 2. test the purity of metals). 'He *assayed* hard to win success' 'He *assayed* the gold ornaments.'
    Essay (a piece of composition). 'Your *essay* is full of grammatical errors.'
13. **Ail** (to be ill). 'He is *ailing* with pneumonia.'
    Ale (a drink). 'He daily goes to the *ale*-house.'

14. **All together** (in a body). 'Let visit him *all together*.'
    Altogether (completely). 'It is *altogether* impossible.'
15. **All ready** (all things or persons are ready). 'We are *all ready* to go to the market.'
    Already (at the moment). 'I have *already* told him.'
16. **Amiable** (lovable). 'His brother is an *amiable* person.'
    Amicable (friendly). 'They stopped the discussion and came to an *amicable* settlement.'
17. **Bale** (package of good). 'I have received four *bales* of cotton.'
    Bail (security). 'He was released on *bail*.'
18. **Berth** (a sleeping place in a train). 'He got reservation for a second-class *berth* in the Punjab Mail.'
    Birth (coming to life). 'The *birth* of a son in a Hindu family is a great event.'
19. **Bare** (uncovered). 'He walks on *bare* foot.'
    Bear (as verb, to carry or to tolerate; as noun, it means a kind of animal). 'The woman *bore* a heavy load on her head.' 'I cannot bear your remarks.' 'Last night in the circus I saw a *bear* riding on a bicycle.'
    Beer (a kind of wine). 'People think that *beer* is good for health.'
20. **Beach** (shore). 'The clash of ripples against the *beach* was a graceful sight.'
    Beech (a kind of tree). 'There is a line of *beech* trees in front of his mansion.'
21. **Bough** (a branch of a tree). 'Birds sit on the *boughs* of trees in my garden and by their sweer notes fill the air with music.'
    Bow (bend). 'Let us *bow* to our motherland.'
22. **Brake** (lever; an instrument to stop a wheel). 'One should not use a bicycle without *brakes*.'
    Break (to make apart). 'You cannot *break* this stick.'
23. **Borrow** (to take on loan). 'We should never *borrow* money from others.'
    Burrow (a hole in earth). 'Serpents live in *burrows*.'
24. **Baron** (a Norman noble: a landlord). 'During the middle Ages all power rested in the hands of rich *barons*.'
    Barren (not fertile; unfruitful). 'It is a bleak and *barren* tract of land.'
25. **Bridal** (pertaining to marriage; adjective of 'bride'). 'She brought to her husband's house many *bridal* presents.'
    Bridle (reins used to drive a horse). 'It is very difficult to *bridle* a vicious horse.'

26. **Calendar** (chart showing the months and days of the year). 'I consult the wall *calendar* almost every day.'
Calender (as verb, 'to press or give finish to a piece of cloth, paper etc.'; as noun, it means a 'roller machine'). '*Calender* my shirt.'

27. **Cannon** (a big gun). 'The sudden roar of *cannons* startled the soldiers.'
Canon (a practice that has become as binding as a law through long usage; a rule). 'One should have a thorough knowledge of all the *canons* of literary criticism before one pronounces judgement on any given work of literature.'

28. **Canvas** (a kind of rough cloth). 'My shoes are made of *canvas*.'
Canvass (to solicit votes). 'During election days, people are seen busy *canvassing* for their candidates.'

29. **Casual** (accidental or occasional). 'In Secretariat fifteen days' *casual* leave is granted to every employee.'
Causal (relating to cause). 'There is no *causal* connection between the miseries of mankind and the position of stars.'

30. **Cast** (as verb, 'to throw'; as noun, it means a list of actors taking part in a play). '*Cast* off your old shoes.' 'The *cast* includes the names of some very famous actors.'
Caste (community). 'He is a Brahmin by *caste*.'

31. **Censer** (a vessel in which incense is burnt in a temple). 'Place the incense into the *censer*.'
Censor (an official examiner of play, films, etc). 'Immoral films must be banned by the *censor*.' 'During war days' all letters were *censored*.'
Censure (disapprove; criticize adversely). 'We should pass a vote of *censure* against the President of our Union.' 'His conduct in the Parliament has been much *censured*.'

32. **Cite** (quote). 'He *cited* many examples from history to prove his argument.'
Site (local position). 'Our college building has a good *site*.'
Sight (view; scene). 'Wordsworth was a great lover of natural scenes and *sights*.'

33. **Check** (1. prevent. 2. test). 'I cannot *check* him from drinking.' 'He *checked* the Railway line and found it satisfactory.'
Cheque (a written order for money to a bank). 'He gave me a bearer *cheque* for Rs. 300.'

34. **Chord** (a string of a musical instrument). 'His violin has fine *chords*.'
Cord (a thin rope). 'Join these *cords* in a knot.'

35. **Career** (profession). 'Shri J. L. Nehru did not achieve any great success in his legal *career*.'
Carrier (one who carries). 'Modern cinema-films are the *carriers* of corruption.'

36. **Coarse** (rough). 'It is a very *coarse* cloth.'
Course (1. way, line of action. 2. each of successive divisions of meal especially soup, fish, mutton and so on). 'I have not yet decided which *course* of life I should adopt.' 'The dinner consisted of twelve *courses*.'

37. **Collision** (clashing; dashing together). In a *collision* between a tram car and a bus, four persons were killed and twenty seriously injured.'
Collusion (secret agreement for an evil purpose). 'The thief was in *collusion* with the servant of the house.'

38. **Corpse** (dead body). 'The *corpse* was covered with wreaths.'
Corps (pronounced as 'kore'; a body of troops). 'National Cadet *Corps* is very useful for young boys and girls.'

39. **Coma** (state of senselessness). 'The patient was in a *coma* for two hours.'
Comma (a mark of punctuation). 'A good writer is always very careful about the use of *commas*.'

40. **Complement** (that which completes). 'Contentment is *complementary* to happiness.'
Compliment (saulte; regards). 'Pay my best *compliments* to you brother.'

41. **Conscious** (aware). 'He is not *conscious* of his weakness.'
Conscientious (honest; careful; scrupulous). 'My new servant is very dutiful and *conscientious*.' 'Pope is a very *conscientious* artist in the use of blank verse.'
Consensus (agreement of opinion). 'There is a wise *consensus* of opinion in our country that Hindi should become our national language.'

42. **Council** (an assembly). 'This bill was passed four years ago in the legislative *council*.'
Counsel (advice). 'Bacon's essays are *counsels*, civil and moral.'

43. **Credible** (believable). 'What you say is hardly *credible*.'
Creditable (worthy of praise). 'His performance of Alexander's role was really very *creditable*.'

IX. DISTINCTION BETWEEN SIMILAR EXPRESSIONS

Sometimes it is seen that a little change or alteration in the position of the simple article 'the' or 'a' or a preposition or a helping verb changes the whole meaning of a sentence. Look at the expressions below:

1. a. **Go to sea** (become a sailor)
   b. **Go to the sea** (go on a voyage)
2. a. **Go to school** (attend school for lessons)
   b. **Go to the school** (for any other purpose).

3. a. **Go to market** (for making purchases)
   b. **Go to the market** (for any other purpose).
4. a. **Go to bed** (go to sleep).
   b. **Go to the bed** (go to the place where the bed is).
5. a. **Go to play** (for the purpose of taking part in the game).
   b. **Go to a** or **the play** (go to a theatre for seeing the acting).
6. a. **Work in hand** (work in which engaged).
   b. **Work on hand** (work not yet done).
7. a. **At no time** (never).
   b. **In no time** (very soon).
8. a. **In an hour** (just after an hour).
   b. **Within in hour** (before the hour is over).
9. a. **In the north** (north but inside; *e.g.*, Pathankot is in the north of India).
   b. **To the north** (north but outside; *e.g.*, Kabul is to the north of India).
10. a. **Work hard** (diligently).
    b. **Work hardly** (scarcely).
11. a. **Little hope of success** (no hope).
    b. **A little hope of success** (some hope at least).
12. a. **Few persons** (none).
    b. **A few person** (some at least).
13. a. **Shot the bird** (killed).
    b. **Shot at the bird** (aimed at the bird for killing).
14. a. **To search a man** (to examine his body and clothes).
    b. **To search for a man** (to find out a man).
15. a. **Believe a man** (believe his statement).
    b. **Believe in a man** (have faith in his honesty).
16. a. **Meet a man** (knowingly)
    b. **Meet with a man** (by chance).
17. a. **Wait for a man** (expect him).
    b. **Wait upon a man** (serve him).
18. a. **A black horse and cow** (a black horse and a black cow).
    b. **A black horse and a cow** (a black horse and a cow which is not black).

19. a. **A neighbour to one** (living near one).
    b. **Neighbour to one** (kind to one)
20. a. **Kalidas** (Kalidas himself).
    b. **A Kalidas** (a poet like Kalidas).
21. a. **Suffer from a headache** (suffer from an occasional attack of headache).
    b. **Suffer from headache** (suffer from a disease, namely headache).
22. a. **The poet and scholar** (one person)
    b. **The poet and the scholar** (two persons).
23. a. **Picture of Ram** (that is the photo of Ram).
    b. **Picture of Ram's** (picture of which Ram is the owner).
24. a. **English** (English language).
    b. **The English** (the English people).
25. a. **Set the book on fire** (burn the book).
    b. **Set the book on the fire** (place the book on the fire).
26. a. **Think little** (to have a poor opinion).
    b. **Little Think** (think scarcely).
27. a. **Come late** (come after fixed time).
    b. **Come lately** (come recently).
28. a. **Go home direct** (go home without stopping anywhere).
    b. **Go home directly** (go home at once)
29. a. **Has come** (coming is finished).
    b. **Is come**(in the state of having come).
30. a. **Is to go** (decided to go).
    b. **Has to go** (under obligation to go).
31. a. **Who is he?** (What is the name of the person?).
    b. **What is he?** (What is the occupation of the person?).
    c. **Which is he?** (Which is he among a group of persons?)
32. a. **The greatest poet** (the greatest poet of all the male and female poets).
    b. **The greatest poetess** (the greatest poet of all the female poets).
33. a. **The eldest son** (the first-born son).
    b. **The oldest son** (the oldest of the living sons).

34. a. **Well** (in good health).
    b. **Well off** (quite rich).
35. a. **A garden flower** (a flower which grows only in gardens).
    b. **A flower garden** (a garden of flowers).
36. a. **Dead in sin** (great sinner).
    b. **Dead to sin** (free from sin).
37. a. **Go before Monday** (go up to Sunday).
    b. **Go by Monday** (go up to Monday).
38. a. **Live at Aligarh** (live in the city of Aligarh).
    b. **Live in Aligarh** (live in the district of Aligarh).
39. a. **Eat fruit** (eat the whole of the fruit).
    b. **Eat of the fruit** (eat a part of the fruit).
40. a. **Live on grass** (feed on grass).
    b. **Live in grass** (live inside the grass).
41. a. **Deal the cards** (distribute the cards).
    b. **Deal in cards** (sell cards)
42. a. **Take heart** (acquire courage).
    b. **Take to heart** (to be deeply affected).
43. a. **Enquire of one** (ask one something).
    b. **Enquire for one** (desire to know one's whereabouts).
44. a. **Stop at Agra** (for some time while going to another place).
    b. **Stop in Agra** (live in Agra temporarily).
45. a. **Want of one** (expect from one).
    b. **Want with one** (to have business with one).
46. a. **At fault** (puzzled).
    b. **In fault** (to blame).
47. a. **Lose one's only son** (to lose one son whom one had).
    b. **Lose one's son only** (to lose one's son and none else).
48. a. **Look sick** (appear to be sick just now).
    b. **Look sickly** (appear to be unhealthy).
49. a. **I have done the work** (I myself have done the work).
    b. **I have the work done** (I have got the work done by somebody else).

50. a. **I can do it** (I can do it, without the help of anybody).

    b. **I alone can do it** (I and nobody else can do it).

51. a. **Was to come** (decided to come).

    b. **Had to come** (obliged to come).

    c. **Was to have come** (did not come, although coming was decided).

52. a. **Arrive home safe** (to be safe when arriving home).

    b. **Arrive home safely** (to have no difficulty on the way).

53. a. **As you are poor** (because you are poor).

    b. **Poor as you are** (although you are poor, yet ...).

54. a. **Seem to be poor** (appear to be poor).

    b. **Seem to have been poor** (appear to have been poor before).

55. a. **Shall die** (destined to die).

    b. **Will die** (determined to die).

56. a. **Be honest** (it implies determination).

    b. **May be honest** (it implies a mere wish).

57. a. **A most interesting play** (interesting in a high degree).

    b. **The most interesting play** (no other is more interesting).

58. a. **The jury was** (the members of the jury taken as a whole).

    b. **The jury were** (the members of the jury taken individually).

59. a. **I would help you if I would** (I would help you if I had the power to help you. I had the will to help you but not the power).

    b. **I could help you if I would** (I could help you if I had a will to help you. I had the power to help you but not the will or intention).

60. a. **A member of society** (one of the human beings who constitute society).

    b. **A member of a society** (a member of a particular association).

61. a. **You love me more than he** (you love me more than he loves me).

    b. **You love me more than him** (you love me more than you love him).

62. a. **Find easy** (find no difficulty in understanding).

    b. **Find easily** (find with no difficulty).

63. a. **Complain to the man** (bring a complaint against the man).

    b. **Complain of the man** (bring a complaint against the man before somebody).

64. a. **Proceed to the work** (being the work).
    b. **Proceed with the work** (resume the work, which had been postponed for a time).
65. a. **See one go** (see one leave the place).
    b. **See one going** (see one when one was on the way).
66. a. **He teaches English as well as writes it** (he teaches English and also writes it).
    b. **He teaches English as well as he writes it** (he teaches and writes English with equal proficiency).
67. a. **Tell me briefly** (tell me in a few words).
    b. **Tell me shortly** (tell me in a short time).
68. a. **Are you going?** (the speaker wants to know whether you are going).
    b. **Are you coming?** (it implies that the speaker is also going).
69. a. **Get drunk** (to become drunk).
    b. **Get drink** (to bring wine).
70. a. **To have regard for** (to have respect for).
    b. **To be regardful of** (to be careful about).
71. a. **Called me** (shouted my name and asked me to come).
    b. **Called on me** (visited me at my house).
72. a. **Being this book** (commence to read this book).
    b. **Begin with this book** (begin this book before beginning any other).
73. a. **Dispense the books** (distribute the books).
    b. **Dispense with the books** (do away with the books).
74. a. **Grasp the chain** (hold the chain tightly).
    b. **Grasp at the chain** (attempt to catch the chain).
75. a. **Guard this man** (protect this man).
    b. **Guard against this man** (take every precaution against this man).
76. a. **Inquire the matter** (ask what the matter is).
    b. **Inquire into the matter** (investigate the matter by careful examination).
77. a. **Repair the house** (put the house in good order).
    b. **Repair to the house** (go to the house).
78. a. **Work the machine** (manage the machine).
    b. **Work at the machine** (be engaged with the machine).

79. a. **Attend the meeting** (to be present in the meeting).
    b. **Attend to the meeting** (to pay attention to the business of the meeting).
80. a. **Come soon** (refers to the time taken in coming and means to come in as short a time as possible).
    b. **Come quickly** (refers to the manner of coming and means, come on as rapid a pace as possible).
81. a. **To have business** (to have a particular affair which demands attention and settlement).
    b. **To have a business** (to have some occupation as a merchant or a shop-keeper).
82. a. **To have enough food** (to have sufficient food).
    b. **To have enough of food** (to have overeaten oneself).
83. a. **Nothing like a battle** (nothing resembling a battle, meaning that the struggle is a trivial affair).
    b. **Nothing like the battle** (meaning that no such battle has occurred before, in other words, the struggle is the most serious).

X. SYNONYMS

The student will do well to familiarize himself with the gradations of words given in the following list. He will find here a good field of discipline for bringing the wealth of English vocabulary within his command. And he may exercise himself profitably upon the same ground by seeking to make further addition to the list.

1. **Assent** (relates to matters of judgement). 'He gave his *assent* on this question.'
   Consent (relates to matters of conduct). 'He gave his *consent* to distribute the prizes.' 'I *consented* to let him go.'
2. **Allow** (denotes a negative action and means 'to abstain from refusal'). 'The students were *allowed* to talk in the class by the teacher.'
   Permit (denotes a positive action and means 'to give a decided assent'). 'He was *permitted* to appear at the B.A. examination.'
3. **Abstain** (from a thing). 'We should *abstain* from wine.'
   Refrain (from action). 'We should *refrain* from drinking.'
4. **Avenge** (to inflict just punishment on evil-doers; it does not imply the gratification of personal grudge, or enmity). 'Hamlet was asked to *avenge* the death of his father.'

Revenge (to inflict pain or injury simply to gratify one's resentment or grudge; it denotes the gratification of personal feeling). 'Francis *revenged* himself upon Hastings by fomenting agitation against him in England.'

5. **Admit** (to acknowledge or concede as true, to give assent to). 'He *admitted* that he was present when the accident took place.'
Confess (not only to concede that a fact is true, but also to acknowledge responsibility or guilt). 'He *confessed* that he had stolen the watch.'

6. **Anger** (a sudden feeling of dispteasure). 'He showed great *anger* at the news.'
Resentment (a more lasting feeling of displeasure). 'My words could not lessen his *resentment*.'

7. **Answer** (a question is answered). 'I *answered* only five questions out of seven set in the paper.'
Reply (a letter or a charge is replied to). 'I sent an immediate *reply* to his letter.'

8. **Attain** (to get by exertion or labour). 'He *attained* a high measure of success in his plan.'
Acquire (to have and hold permanently). 'Recently, he has *acquired* a thorough knowledge of Botony.'

9. **Ancient** (opposed to modern). 'There is not much material available about the *ancient* history of India.'
Old (opposed to new and to young). 'The *old* edition of this book is not available in the market.' '*Old* people prefer simplicity to show.'

10. **Ability** (power to do something; skill in the use of physical powers or intellectual faculties; Ability is developed through exercise). 'Men are promoted on the basis of the *ability* that they show.' 'He has unusual *ability* as a mechanic.'
Capacity (power to achieve, hold or contain; as applied to intellectual faculties *capacity* means power to take in knowledge as distinguished from power to express it in doing. It usually implies inborn power as power distinguished from that which is acquired). 'His *capacity* for Mathematics is very limited.'

11. **Astonishment** (extreme surprise; implies some degree of perplexity or confusion). 'I was *astonished* to see him begging on the roadside.'
Surprise (arises on the occurrence of something new or unexpected). 'Your failure in the examination has *surprised* me.'
Wonder (surprise mingled with admiration or curiosity). 'We *wonder* at the skill of those who built the Taj.'

12. **Bravery** (lies in the blood and depends on the physical environment. 'The brave man does not reason and reflect: he rushes in to the battle into the thick of the fight and finds his joy in the tumult of the battle). 'The *bravery* of the English gave them victory over the indolent and luxurious Nawabs of Bengal.'
Courage (lies in the mind and is a matter of reason and reflection. It is a result of man's character and conviction. It is a lofty sentiment). 'He has the *courage* to speak out his mind.' 'In the hour of crisis his *courage* failed him.'
Valour (is a higher quality than either bravery or courage and possesses the grand characteristics of both. The man who possesses valour forms great projects and is ready to risk his life for glory). 'The knights of King Arthur's court were known for their deeds of *valour*.'
Boldness (is usually short-lived, suggestive of rising to the occasion). 'He showed *boldness* in fighting the fire.'
Daring (suggests rashness and is venturesome). 'He is *daring* but not prudent, that is why he ventures to do things which no wise man would ever do.'
13. **Battle** (a single contest between two opposing armies). 'The third *battle* of Panipat gave a death-blow to the Mughal Empire.'
War (a series of contests between opposing armies continued for a long time). 'The German militarism was crushed in the last Great *War*.'
Fight (a combat between a small number of persons). 'Many were wounded and a few killed in the *fight* between the students and the police.'
14. **Begin** (used on all occasions). 'The sooner you *begin* the work, the earlier you finish it.'
Commence (used only in official and formal language). 'The examinations will *commence* on the 5th of July.'
Start (implies an idea of an actual physical motion). 'The train *starts* at 10 o'clock.'
15. **Beautiful** (implies certain degree of delicacy which makes it inapplicable to man; for whom the only terms of admiration are, 'handsome' and 'fine'). 'She is the most *beautiful* girl of our village.'
Handsome (is used for man, or for the beauty of some person or thing that is trained or cultivated). 'He is a *handsome* body of twenty.' 'It is a very *handsome* horse.'
16. **Custom** (generally refers to the repeated action of many persons, a community, a society, a race, etc.). 'It is the *custom* of the British to be honest in their business dealings.'
Habit (is applicable when we are speaking of just person). 'It is her *habit* to do the cooking early in the morning.'

17. **Cite** (is used for things or persons). 'He *cited* the authority of the Quran.' 'It is advisible to *cite* no one whose authority is likely to be challenged.'
Quote (is used for things only). 'He *quoted* passage after passage from Milton.'

18. **Compulsion** (is physical; we are compelled to do what is generally against our wishes). 'He was *compelled* by the court to be present on that day.'
Obligation (is moral; we are obliged to do what is imposed on us as a duty). 'We are *obligated* to maintain those who depend on us.'

19. **Confer** (conferring is an act of authority). 'The government *confers* titles on eminent persons.'
Bestow (bestowing is an act of generosity or charity). 'Many presents were *bestowed* on the refugees.'

20. **Crime** (an offence against the law on the State). 'It is a *crime* to go into a stranger's house at night.'
Vice (an offence against morals). 'Drinking is a *vice*.'
Sin (an offence against the law of God or religious law). 'It is a *sin* to tell a lie.'

21. **Ceiling** (the inner part of a roof). 'A lamp is hanging from the *ceiling*.'
Roof (the entire covering of a room or house). 'They are flying kites on the *roof* of their house.'

22. **Character** (mental or moral nature). 'A man of *character* overcomes all temptations.'

23. **Contentment** (a state of mind in which one does not wish for more). 'Happiness consists in *contentment*.'
Satisfaction (fulfillment of one's expectations). 'The principal is not *satisfied* with his work.' 'He completed the work to my entire *satisfaction*.'

24. **Contagious** (used for a disease which is caught by contact). 'Smallpox is a *contagious* disease.'
Infectious (used for a disease which is spread through air or water). 'Malaria is an *infectious* disease.'

25. **Cool** (denotes an unpleasant sensation). 'India is a land of fertile toil and *cool* breezes.'
Cold (denotes an unpleasant sensation). 'It is very *cold* this evening.'

26. **Defend** (refers to present danger). 'The Rajputs heroically *defended* the for t against the assault of the Mughal army.'
Protect (refers to approaching danger). 'An umbrella *protects* the body from sun and shower.'

27. **Deny** (refers to matters of fact of knowledge, and therefore, we deny as to the past. A denial affects our veracity or truthfulness). 'The prisoner *denied* the charge that had been brought against him.' 'He *denied* is participation in the meeting held on Sunday last.'
Refuse (refers to matters of wish or request, and therefore, we refuse as to he future. 'Refuse' is generally followed by an infinitive. A refusal affects our good nature). 'He *refused* to lend me his book.'

28. **Doubt** (to doubt's fact or a statement is to be inclined to think it untrue). 'I *doubt* his honesty (*i.e.,* I am inclined to think that he is not honest.'
Suspect (to suspect is to be inclined to think a thing true). 'The police *suspect* him to be a thief (*i.e.,* the police are inclined to think that he is a thief).'

29. **Discover** (to find out a thing or country that existed before). 'Captain Scott *discovered* the South Pole.'
Invent (to create what did not exist before). 'George Stephenson *invented* the locomotive engine.'

30. **Drown** (refers to persons). 'Do not bathe in deep water or you will *drown.*'
Sink (refers to things). 'The ship dashed against a rock and *sank.*'

31. **Desire** (is used of that which is near at hand or in thought). 'We *desire* wealth, distinction, honour, fame etc.'
Wish (is used of that which is remote). 'I *wish* I were a bird so that I could fly to you.'
Want(is used of that which is lacking or absent). 'I *want* many things but I need only a few of them.'
Need (is used of that which is both lacking and necessary) 'I want my *needs* to be fulfilled.'
Require (demand or ask in words). 'Your presence is *required* there.'

32. **Envy** (feeling uneasy at others' good fortune). 'He is *envious* of his sister's wealth.'
Jealousy (a passion to possess or retain what is our own). 'The citizens were *jealous* of their ancient privileges.'

33. **Enough** (relates to the quantity which one wishes to have of anything; all that one wants). 'For a miser nothing is *enough.*'
Sufficient (relates to the use that is to be made of anything all that one needs). 'In Russia, every citizen is provided with as much as is *sufficient* for his healthy living.'

34. **Event** (an important happening). 'The defeat of Rana Sanga was a great *event* in the history of India.'

Incident (an ordinary happening). 'Our local newspapers give us a detailed account of daily *incidents*.'
Accident (an unexpected occurrence). 'These days can *accidents* are common.'

35. **Excuse** (is use with reference to trifling matters). 'You will *excuse* my meeting you at this odd hours.'
Forgive (is used with reference to give offences). 'To err is human, to *forgive* divine.'
Pardon (is used with reference to simpler offences). 'I beg your *pardon*.'

36. **Famous** (is used in a good sense). 'Paris is *famous* for its cafes and hotels.'
Notorious (is used in a bad sense). 'He is a *notorious* drunkard.'
Renowned (is used for a high and dignified kind of reputation). 'Dr. Radharkrishnan is a *renowned* scholar.'

37. **Freedom** (implies absence of restraint at the present moment). 'The English people enjoy a *freedom* which no other nation possessess.'

38. **Liberty** (implies previous restraint). 'The prisoner was set at *liberty*.'

39. **Falsehood** (something said or done with or without the idea of deceiving a man). 'He was guilty of *falsehood* when he spoke against the character and culture of the Indians.'
Lie (speak untrue words with the intention of deceiving others). 'He was punished for telling a *lie*.'

40. **Grateful** (one who makes a return for the kindness of a benefactor is 'grateful': it refers to conduct). 'We should always be *grateful* to those who help us in need.'
Thankful (one who cherishes the memory of the favours shown by one's benefactor is thankful: it refers to state of mind). 'We should be *thankful* to our friends.'

41. **Hope** (is used when we anticipate is welcome, and not against, our wishes). 'Even the most incompetent lawyer *hopes* to succeed.'